Dec 25, 1993

Merry Christmas
Elly & Drew!

Irene & Jay
(The Blakeneys of Borneo)

# SARAWAK
## Style

# SARAWAK
## *Style*

LUCA INVERNIZZI TETTONI
EDRIC ONG

TIMES EDITIONS

*Page 1: A beaded panel from the back of a baby carrier depicting two masked spirits entwined with four hornbill heads.*

*Page 2: The* baruk *or headhouse of the Bidayuh people has a conical* nipah *palm thatch roof with a bird effigy perched at the apex.*

*Pages 6-7: Early morning scene along the Delok River. An Iban elder with his hunting dog negotiates a river in his dugout canoe.*

*Sarawak offers a wealth of natural life. Page 8: (Clockwise from top right) The fragrant and delicate orchid Catasetum; Bidayuh forest ranger with the Rafflesia, world's largest flower; pitcher plant at Gunung Murud; wild jungle flower; Usun Apau Waterfalls; Limestone Pinnacle of Batu Lawi.*
*Centre: Forest fungi.*

*Page 9: (Clockwise from top right) Lantern bug; damselfly; rhinoceros hornbill; pit viper; Hormurus wood scorpion; sambar deer; Bornean orang-utan; mossy plank buttresses of the tropical rainforest; mimicry phasmid insect.*

Photo Credits: Max Lawrence/Photobank, pages 8-9; Larry Tackett/Photobank, page 9 (bottom, far left)

## ACKNOWLEDGEMENTS

This book would not have been possible without the sponsors and the support of many people, to whom the author and photographer are grateful.

We would specially like to thank the Staff of Edric Ong Architects who arranged for most of the homes and resorts to be photographed as well as made drawings for the architectural notebook; and to Nelson Tan of Nelson's Gallery who kindly provided items from his collections for photography.

Our thanks go to:
Y.A. Bhg Datuk Amar Puan Sri (Dr) Hajjah Laila Taib, Y.B. Tan Sri Datuk Amar Alfred Jabu and Puan Sri Datin Paduka Empiang Jabu, Y.B. Datuk Dr George Chan, Y.B. Datuk Adenan Satem, Y.B. Dr James Masing, Tuan Haji Abdillah Haji Abdul Rahim, Rt Rev. Bishop Made Katib, Rt Rev. Bishop John Leong, Y. Bhg Datuk Robert Jacob Ridu and Datin Garnette Ridu, Y.B. Datuk Effendi Norwawi and Datin Farida, Datin Amar Margaret Linggi, Datuk Lucas Chin, Puan Deanna Ibrahim, Dr Peter Kedit of Sarawak Museum, Mr Aloysius Dris, Mr Philip Ting of CMS, Encik Shamshir Salleh Askor and Staff of Holiday Inn Damai Beach, Miss Lily Dublin of Kuching Hilton, Manager and Staff of Batang Ai Hilton, Manager and Staff of Pelagus Rapids Resort, Puan Jane Lian Labang and Staff of Sarawak Cultural Village, Mr Philip Yong of Borneo Adventure, Mr and Mrs Ong Kee Bian, Miss Edwina Ong, Mr Yap Han Boon of Reddi & Co, Mr Wee Hong Seng, Mr Henry Ho and Mr Richard Chan of Fabriko, Mr Lim Yu Seng (photographer) and Staff of Sarawak Museum, Mr Michael Lim, Mr Gerald Jabu, Ms Magdalene Tai, Mr Roger Aninag, Mr Peter Chia of Atelier, Mr Tay Peng Huat, Mr Dennis Lau, Mr Lim Poh Chiang, Ms Alice Lim and Mr Stanley Paran.

Last, but not least, we would like to thank Ms Shirley Hew, Mr Tan Kok Eng and Mr Tuck Loong of Times Editions.

SARAWAK STYLE



Published by Times Editions
an imprint of Times Editions Pte Ltd
Times Centre, 1 New Industrial Road
Singapore 536196

Publisher: Shirley Hew
Project Editor: KE Tan
Art Director: Tuck Loong
Production Manager: Anthoney Chua
Colour separation by Colourscan Co. Pte Ltd, Singapore
Printed by KHL Printing Co Pte Ltd



ISBN 981 204 648 8

# CONTENTS

# INTRODUCTION

*Left: The Usun Apau Waterfalls lies amidst the verdant green of Sarawak's stunning rainforest.*

*Above, top and bottom: Watercolour of Rajah Brooke's garden and pitcher plants, both painted in 1851 by Harriette MacDougall.*

Man began living in the Great Niah Caves of Sarawak some 40,000 years ago. Later, they built shelters in the jungle which evolved into longhouses. Today, life in Sarawak speaks of a style unique to the land and its multiracial people.

Located on northwestern Borneo, the world's third largest island, Sarawak has fascinated early explorers and adventurers. The tourism slogans "World's Best-Kept Secret", "Land of Hornbills", "Land of Longhouses" inadequately describe this land of luxuriant equatorial rainforests and its equally rich indigenous culture comprising the twenty-five and more races of Sarawak.

Sarawak is not a country locked up in the history of time. A blue-jean and T-shirt cladded youth riding a motorbike is more the daily sight today rather than a young warrior in loincloth carrying a blowpipe.

The capital city of Kuching and other main towns have their fair share of high-rise, high-tech modern buildings and five-star hotels. Yet contrasting with that, half an hour's journey away, are thatch-roofed villages, longhouses and forests along meandering rivers amidst mountain ranges.

A land that has been little known except by barter traders from China in the 10th century A.D. in search of jungle products like camphor, beeswax, resin (dammar), rhinoceros horn and hornbill ivory, Sarawak first came under the influence of the Buddhist Srivijaya Empire in the 7th century based in South Sumatra, then by the Hindu Majapahit Empire which originated in Java. With the decline of Majapahit in the 15th century, Sarawak became the southern province of the sultanate of Brunei, one of the most important centres of Islam and one of the great sea states of the Malay Archipelago.

Formal recorded history of Sarawak started in 1839 with the arrival of James Brooke who established the state and reigned as Rajah. His descendants, Charles and Charles Vyner Brooke, continued the Raj till the Japanese Occupation in 1941.

For indigenous cultures that had existed independently for several millenia, the arrival of the first Brooke 166 years ago, and the political changes that ensued from British Colonial rule (1945 -1963) to national independence within Malaysia (since 1963) has irrevocable effects. The plight of the remaining 500 or so nomadic Penan in the Sarawak rainforests today becomes a tussle between the politics of development and the traditions of a lifestyle that has survived from the past.

In the last century, Sarawak attracted a fair share of explorers, naturalists, historians and artists. Volumes of books by Hugh Low, Beccari and Charles Hose are now invaluable anthro-

*Above: Sir James Brooke, the first "White Rajah".*

*Right: Old prints depict the Brunei Sultanate (top) and the Sultan's Audience Hall (bottom) in the 1860s.*

pological and archival material of the indigenous people, some of whom are now extinct, like the Ukits. In 1855, the compatriot of Darwin, Alfred Russell Wallace spent some time in the jungles of Sarawak to derive his own viewpoint on the theory of evolution. Similarly, Somerset Maugham's short stories of Sarawak lent a "romantic" flavour to the country.

The early watercolour paintings of Sarawak by Harriette MacDougall, the first Anglican Bishop's wife in 1840s, and the oil paintings by Marian North in the 1870s (now in the Kew Gardens Gallery in London) have captured for us the tranquil beauty of Sarawak's lush landscape of mountains, rivers, jungles, fruits, orchids and insects. Other visiting artists of the era have come in search of "the noble savage"; found them and recorded them in style on lithographs and wood prints.

What attracted these artists was the remarkable diversity of Sarawak's landscape from the coastal plains and swamps to the mountain ranges in the interior. The two highest peaks, Gunong Murud and Gunong Mulu, stand at a height of 2,450 metres and 2,376 metres respectively. Massive limestone formations at the Mulu National Park are among the most spectacular in the world, as are the famous Mulu Caves discovered during a Royal Geographical Society expedition in the 1980s.

Meandering through all this landscape, the mighty rivers of the Rejang, Baram and Batang Lupar pour their waters into the sea. Here and there along the way, waterfalls, oxbow lakes and rapids are formed. The main rivers are tidal, with vast drops in level, depending also on rainfall. They still serve as the main mains of transport in Sarawak.

The average rainfall is 2,500 mm and average day temperature hovers around 27°C. There is no distinct dry and wet seasons; the seasons are described generally as "wet" and "wetter" for the *landas* months between November and February when the northeast monsoon winds blow.

One of the world's most complex and luxuriant rainforests are found in Sarawak. The interior dipterocarp forest, found up to 1,200 metres above sea level, is the backbone of the state timber industry which is the second most important economic resource after oil and gas. In the alluvial plains of the lowlands, another riverine forest is found. This is the home of the famous *belian* or ironwood much esteemed by all people for its durable qualities for house construction. Towards the coastal lowland, peat swamp forests dominate.

The physical landform with its remarkable diversity of swampy coastal land, interspersed with rivers, impenetrable jungles, precipitous mountains have separated the indigenous people into small communities, each living in its own domain of river systems, valleys or high plateaus, their private "Shangri-La".

Intertribal wars and clashes were part of the past survival instinct and headhunting was a spiritual excursion. All these practices came to an end under the Brooke regime of law and order. Great battles had been fought against marauding pirates and dissenting warfaring tribes along the river systems from 1843 to 1850 . The last heads were reckoned to have been taken during the Japanese surrender in 1945.

Today, the dark reminders of those perilous days are the old soot-covered skulls hanging in the longhouses – trophies of an ancient past – and the old weapons of wars, the parangs and spears.

Life in the jungle can be easy or hard. The jungle can be a friend or a foe, a provider of food but also teeming with other creepy crawlies and animals. The hot, wet and humid weather can be unbearable to the unaccustomed, but its consistency all year round can be an asset.

The indigenous people's response to this environment has been one of a harmonious understanding of the ecosystem passed down from their ancestors. Customs and traditions interwoven with the old religions often spell out the rules and guidelines for a lifestyle centred around padi-culture and survival in the rainforests.

There is a quiet understanding of living in harmony with the environment, a respect for the elements of nature. Like Adam in the Garden of Eden, man was not meant to be an intruder in the rainforests, but to coexist in it, loving and caring for God's creation even as he too is part of it.

In Sarawak, there are no great stone temples from the past like Borobudur in Java or Angkor Wat in Cambodia – no architectural wonders that had withstood the ravages of time. Architectural forms and habitat were made of the same material as the forest environment itself and if not recycled and re-used, the man-built structure once abandoned is claimed back by the forest quite rapidly.

Perhaps the summary of the temporal nature of Sarawak style is a strong reminder to us that we are but pilgrims and sojourners in this world.

*Above: A native war dance in lino-print.*

*Left and below: Headhunting was a spiritual excursion and the result of intertribal warfare. Trophy skulls hang on display in the longhouse gallery.*

First Iban Girl To Graduate As B.A.
THE SARAWAK TRIBUNE
NEW ZEALAND
TAN SRI DATUK AMAR ALFRED
DEPUTY CHIEF

# PEOPLE, HERITAGE AND CULTURE

*Preceding page: The Iban people at the Peace-Keeping Ceremony, 1898.*

*Above: For the Iban, the rifle became as much a symbol of bravery and manhood as the* parang ilang *swords they traditionally carry.*

*Opposite: Photographs from the family of Tan Sri Datuk Amar Alfred Jabu reflect the progressive nature of most Iban families in education, politics and society at large.*

The early people of Sarawak in prehistoric times (25,000 - 45,000 years ago, Upper Pleistocene period) lived in the Great Niah Cave. Archaeologists and scientists postulate that the island of Borneo together with Sumatra, Java and the Palawan Island of the Philippines were land-linked to mainland Asia through the Sunda Shelf. This provided a way for the migration of people (Australoids) and animals to the Southeast Asian islands from the mainland.

What became of the Sarawak Man, and who their descendants are is still the speculation of anthropologists today.

In present-day Sarawak, there are more than 25 ethnic communities within a population of 1.8 million. The main groups are: Iban (29.6%), Chinese (29.1%), Malay (20.7%), Bidayuh (8.3%), Melanau (5.8%), Orang Ulu (5.4%), and others including Indians (1.1 %)

Colonial historians used the term "Dayaks" to denote all non-Muslim indigenous people. Today, it is preferred to use the name Iban instead of Sea Dayak, and Bidayuh instead of Land Dayak. All the indigenous people are now categorised as "Bumiputera" under the national law of Malaysia.

The multi-ethnicity of the state is therefore an interesting blend of diverse cultural and religious heritage, a political melting pot that has been simmered to a harmonious brew. Sarawakians take pride in being Sarawakians, and the sentiments remain strong although Sarawak became a state of Malaysia 32 years ago in 1963.

Culturally, Sarawak is more akin to the rest of Borneo, i.e. Kalimantan Indonesia, Sabah and Brunei rather than Peninsular Malaysia. In a land where the average population density is 10.4 per square kilometre, it is still considered a land of plenty, and of opportunity.

Perhaps, it is the open country atmosphere and the prevalence of a civil attitude towards work, play and life in general that gives Sarawak that friendly ambience. However, the peace and order of today was not established without blood, sweat and tears. James Brooke's arrival in 1839 was to settle a revolt by the Malays and Bidayuh against Makota, the Brunei Sultan's governor. In the ensuing years, as Rajah, several battles had to be fought against pirates and feuding tribes. With the establishment of a strong government administration, economic development followed.

Although there is a conscious effort to evolve a national culture as it has been in establishing the national language Bahasa Malaysia, the strong roots of each individual's ethnic heritage still maintain their separate cultural identity and integrity. Perhaps only time will erase the cultural exclusivity and give birth to a cross-cultural hybrid that would be termed Sarawakian or Malaysian.

*This page: A traditional welcome to a longhouse involves a* miring *ceremony, the making of offerings to the spirits for a harmonious visit. The man's* ngajat *dance (top left) depicts his exploits in the jungle, but it is the ladies' costumes of silver (top right, centre and bottom) that catch the eye.*

*Opposite: Tuai-Rumah Along, Iban chief of the Nanga Sumpa longhouse holds his pet fighting cockerel.*

# IBAN

The biggest ethnic group, with almost half a million, the Iban moved from the Kapuas River basin in Kalimantan to the Ulu Ai areas of Sarawak some 40 generations ago. Fiercely protective of their river systems where they settled, they identified themselves as Kami Saribas and Kami Krian or "we of the Saribas River" and "we of the Krian River". The majority still live in longhouses along the main rivers and tributaries on the lowland plains, although a great number live in the urban towns working in the civil service or in the business sector.

Being riverine people, the Iban are skilful in making large longboats. In days of tribal aggression, the war boats can fill up to 40 to 50 men. Their traditional religion is animistic and embraces a spirit world of mystical deities and legendary heroes. Dreams and bird augury, taboos, customs and rituals were part and parcel of life in a longhouse.

Many festivals or *gawai* mark their calendar year. There is Gawai Kenyalang which commemorates the bravery of warriors, Gawai Antu which is held to appease the dead souls and Gawai Batu, which is celebrated before the rice-planting season.

The official Harvest Festival, Gawai Dayak, held on June 1st, is the biggest celebration however. It is during this time that Kumang Gawai or "Harvest Princess" is selected from the community. Fair maidens from the various Iban districts are dressed in their finest costume and silver to parade in a dazzling display of beauty and wealth. Fond as they are of revelry, the Iban on such occasions brew a rice wine called *tuak* and perform the *ngajat* dance to an accompaniment of a brass xylophone instrument, the *engkaromong*.

The Iban are also famous for their splendid warp-*ikat* weave called *pua kumbu*, a "spiritual" cloth closely associated with their mystical old religion and the past practice of headhunting.

Cock-fighting is a favourite sport among the Iban. In many longhouses, these prized cockerels will be the subject of much care and attention among the menfolk.

The traditional Iban way of life is very communal and democratic. Living in a longhouse, each family occupies a standard size room, a *bilik*. They elect their own headman or Tuai Rumah. Several headmen from the longhouse of an area or river system would elect their own chief known as *penghulu*. All posts are not hereditary and even if the choice of leadership may fall on the elderly chief's son, he must still be elected.

LONGHOUSE CHIEF FLIES
IN NAVY 'COPTER
TENTERA UDARA DIRAJA MALAYSIA
SENTIASA DI-ANGKASA RAYA

# BIDAYUH

Formerly known as Land Dayak, because they lived in the hilly areas outside of Kuching, the Bidayuh comprise several distinct subgroups: Bukar/Sadong (Serian District); Biatah (Kuching District); Singgai (Bau District); Jagoi (Bau District); Lara and Selakau (Lundu District). Their dialects are different, but related. Costumes are predominantly black and red in colour, but may vary according to dialect groups.

Originally animistic in belief, the Bidayuh were among the first to be converted by the Protestant missionaries in the 1850s. Most Bidayuh practise shifting cultivation of padi on hilly farmland. Today, many educated Bidayuh work in offices and factories in the towns.

Paka anak Otor is the Tua Gawai or "Ritual Chief" of Kampong Benuk, 33 kilometres from Kuching in the Penrissen Hills. For 12 generations, his family has been ritual chiefs starting with Karang, followed by Pasi, Iteng, Barow, Nijah, Sambu, Rugah, Maren, Riguh, Sunjan and Otor.

*Above: Ritual chief Paka anak Otor poses in ceremonial attire in front of an old British colonial flag of Sarawak.*

*Left: Family photographs and mementos decorate a corner of Paka anak Otor's house. The ceremonial carved bamboo stick on the right is his instrument of authority as ritual chief.*

*Top left: Pa' Sijan's family from Kampong Pichin wear the traditional Bidayuh red and black costumes during festive occasions.*

*Top right: St. James Church in the Bidayuh village of Quop was built in 1865 and has a fine heritage of choral singing.*

*Above: Kumbu ak Katau is a Bidayuh carver of Christian icons in his spare time. His family are cocoa and hill padi farmers in the Serian District.*

*Opposite: Grace Tony Weng, a 15-year-old Kelabit student in traditional beaded cap and heirloom necklaces poses with a prized Kenyah sunhat.*

From stories handed down, it is known that his ancestor, Karang, lived in a limestone cave called Kibuo near the Pang Creek, a tributary of the Benuk River.

In his little house museum, Paka continues to tell the stories of days gone by when Kampong Benuk was still the largest longhouse in the district. The visit of the British naval sailors of *HMS Thankerton* in 1966 was well recorded in photo albums; so was his father Otor's first helicopter ride, which was published in a local newspaper.

Times have changed, but memories linger on to be shared with the younger generations.

## ORANG ULU

The name refers collectively to all the peoples of the interior of Sarawak, including the larger groups such as the Kayan, Kenyah, Kelabit, Lun Bawang, and the smaller groups such as the Bisaya, Kejaman, Sekapan, Lahanan, Sihan, Ukit and Penan.

Generally living in the interior and upland part of the country, most of the Orang Ulu groups are related to the tribal people of Kalimantan Borneo.

The Kayan and the Kenyah originated from the Apo-Kayan, the upper reaches of the Kayan River in Kalimantan. They moved into their present area several hundred years ago.

Previously animistic, most Orang Ulu are now staunch Christians. Many Kelabit and Lun Bawang attained high education, although wet-padi cultivation is very much the main occupation of the majority in the highland plains.

Among the Lun Bawang and Kelabit, the *kerbau* or buffalo is highly-prized and valued. Dowry for a bride is at least seven buffaloes for the upper class, and includes heirloom jars, antique beads and baskets.

Fair in complexion, and stocky in build, most Orang Ulu are adapt in traversing the hills and mountains while carrying heavy loads.

Traditionally, the Kayan and Kenyah women have extended earlobes weighed down by heavy brass rings. They have finely patterned tattoos on their forearms and legs. Men and women alike removed their eyebrows and eyelashes to enhance a smooth complexion.

*Right: Long earlobes were considered a thing of beauty among the Kenyah and Kayan women. At a young age, the ears are pierced and drop earrings worn to stretch the lobes. This Kenyah woman is decked out in solid brass, fruit-shaped ear weights.*

*Below: Temenggong Oyong Lawai Jau (at centre), the paramount Kenyah chief in Sarawak, poses with his two Iban friends.*

The Orang Ulu has a social hierarchy system: a lower, middle, and an upper class which is hereditary. As a result of the class system imbued in them, they have great respect for their chiefs. In the longhouse, the chief occupies a larger apartment in a central position while the other villagers are spread out on either side, decreasing in social standing as they become further removed from the Chief's Unit.

Having given up their headhunting practices decades ago, the Orang Ulu are generally considered a gentle people whose cultural traditions include the graceful dance of the *kanjet*, performed to simulate hornbill birds in flight, and music played on a four-string lute called *sape*.

The Orang Ulu are all gifted singers. They are very musical, sing in harmony and have melodious voices. Their songs relate a legend or the fabulous virtues of a visitor. A man or a woman sings the refrain and everyone joins in the chorus singing in harmony.

## MELANAU

Living in kampong settlements along the coast and estuary of the Rejang River, the Melanau traditionally were fishermen and producers of the sago-palm flour.

Some ancient communities used to live in longhouse-type tall houses built on stilts. Today, none of such structures remain. The Melanau through their assimilation of a Malay lifestyle have adopted the separate stilt-house habitat.

Their old religion is Liko, meaning "people of the river", although many are now Christians and Muslims. Liko relates to nature; that life is harmoniously interwoven with the environment. Their spiritual world embraces superior *tou* spirits and the lesser *belum* spirits that cause sickness and trouble. Pagan Melanau practise a system of traditional healing called *berbayuh* and *berayun*, using effigies of sickness spirits called *belum* carvings.

Specially carved bone fetishes are attached to the nets by the fishermen and annually a *kaul* festival is celebrated on the beach to bless the fishing season.

Educated Melanau today occupy prominent positions in the government and business community of the State.

*Above: Tusau Padan, a well-known Kenyah master artist, paints his unique designs on the sape (a stringed wooden instrument), while his wife looks on. He is also an accomplished musician and dancer, and an expert in blowpipe shooting.*

*Far left: A Melanau shaman making his belum healing effigies.*

*Near Left: Malike Mahli is the architect of the Kuching City North Council. His family still reside in their kampong house at Oya, Dalat.*

*Left: Traditional dressing is kept alive especially during the Hari Raya festival. Elyna Effendi wears the classic* selayah *headscarf of hand-embroidered silver threads and an heirloom gold-woven traditional Malay dress.Her antique gold necklace is a Melanau heirloom.*

*Opposite: Bright-coloured curtains contrast with the dullness of an unpainted timber wall. Almost all Malay kampong houses have curtained windows, more for decoration than privacy.*

# THE MALAY

Living along the coast and in villages along the river banks, the ethnic background of the Sarawak Malay is diverse depending on where their ancestors came from – Sumatra, Java or Kalimantan Borneo. Despite differences in customs and social etiquette, their Muslim faith unites the community.

Kampong or village communal living is still the norm. Even as housing estates are now developed, the Malay would choose to stay close together, particularly among relatives.

Moral, marital, social and monetary disputes are settled by Muslim Syariah courts, and every small village have their *surau* prayer halls.

The main annual celebration is Hari Raya Puasa which marks the end of the fasting month of Ramadan. Every family holds an open house to welcome relatives and friends.

It is every Muslim Malay's aspiration to make their pilgrimage to Mecca, the holy city at least once in their life. Having accomplished that, the men can wear white caps for prayers in place of the standard black *songkok* hats.

The Malay love for colour and ornaments is evident in their homes and in their dressing. Wedding ceremonies *bersanding* are elaborate. The bridal couple are "enthroned" on a specially carved bed and showered with blessings of scented water and *tepung tawar* petals by elders and guests.

A *hadrah* tambourine group greets the arrival of the bridegroom, and in the evening the women play the *gendang* drums while the men dance the *joget* amongst themselves throughout the night. Well-known Malay songs are sung by the women to the strong rhythm of the drums, but they never dance. A low curtain stretched across the room separates the women from the men. Occasionally the men would flirt with the girls by singing the *pantun* or poetic songs.

Traditional medicine is still practised in the kampong or villages. A specialty of Lundu Malays is mixing fine slices of the bud of the Rafflesia giant flower with other spices. This is much valued by pregnant women.

Among their culinary skills, the Malays are known for their satay, little pieces of savoury beef or chicken grilled on palm frond skewers over a charcoal fire and eaten with *ketupat* rice-cake and a hot and appetising sauce of ground-up peanuts. The Malays also have a few types of curry, less chilli hot than the Indian version because more coconut milk is used.

*Top: A Chinese family photograph taken at a picnic outing during the turn of the century. The nyonya ladies in the picture are dressed in* sarong kebaya, *Malay-style.*

*Bottom: A Hokkien Association committee meeting is chaired by the late Mr Ong Kwan Hin. The street outside bears the name of his grandfather, Ong Ewe Hai.*

*Opposite: The merchant Chinese were well educated and Western-influenced, particularly in their dressing as seen in these photographs from the Ong family.*

# THE CHINESE

Trade between China and the Sarawak people date back to the 10th-century Tang dynasty, as evidenced by ceramics excavated at the Sarawak River delta. Camphor, beeswax, bird's nests, hornbill ivory and other exotic products were traded for textiles, beads, ceramics and brassware.

By the 1 840s when James Brooke arrived, there was already a thriving Chinese community in Kuching. As peace and order was established, more Chinese merchants and farmers were encouraged to come.

The many dialect groups of the Chinese include Hokkien, Teochew, Hakka, Foochow, Heng-hua, Chawan and Cantonese. Those who came from mainland China brought their culture with them. Others whose ancestors were already settlers of the Straits Settlements like Malacca, Penang and Singapore had assimilated the local Malay culture and were known as Peranakan Chinese: baba (for the men), nyonya (for the ladies). The nyonya wore *sarong kebaya*, adopted from the Malay.

The traditional belief of the Chinese is a blend of Taoist-Buddhist-Confucian philosophy. Dialect groups brought their patron saints or deities with them and set up temples and clanhouses.

Every Chinese celebrate the Chinese Lunar New Year with much festivity that lasts fifteen days. The traditional lion dance and other pugilistic arts are still practised.

The Moon Cake Festival is celebrated on the fifteenth day of the eight Lunar Month. Multi-coloured lanterns in the shape of fish, flowers, birds, etc, are lit and carried by children. Round moon cakes with sweet lotus and bean paste fillings are exchanged between families as symbols of thanksgiving and happiness.

Through the years, there have been intermarriages between the different dialect groups and also with other ethnic races. The early Chinese settlers set up their own "Chung Hua" schools with Mandarin as the medium of education. With the implementation of the Federal education system, these schools have now become bilingual, with Bahasa Malaysia being taught as the first language.

A major part of the commercial trading in Sarawak is still done by the Chinese and of recent years the emergence of the timber industry has been led by the Foochows. It is said that where there is money to be made, you will find a Chinese there. Even in the most remote of riverine towns like Belaga or Engkilili, there are small shophouses that form a bazaar. Barter trade was the old practice with the indigenous people. It is becoming less of a norm today. Most of these shopkeepers speak the local ethnic language fluently and over the decades have built up relationships of mutual trust and confidence with their native neighbours.

In the arts and crafts, Chinese potters have since their arrival set up their dragon kilns to produce ceramic urns and other wares for local use. In the 1970s, native Dayak designs were incorporated into the ceramics and this started a "Borneo Pottery" identity. Replicas of the old heirloom Chinese dragon jars continue to be made to meet the demands of the Iban and Bidayuh.

The entrepreneurial aptitude of the Chinese as they absorb the local ethnic culture is evident not only in the way in which the pottery kilns have now infused tribal motifs into their ceramic waves, but also in the way Sarawak souvenirs, T-shirts and printed textiles are being marketed.

*Above left: Seventy-two-year-old Sim Yam Phua is the third generation to run the Buan Choon Tng (literally "Million Years' Shop") Chinese pharmacy at China Street.*

*Left: The traditional dragon kiln at Ng Li Seng pottery.*

# Malaysian cat city boasts feline museum

By Reme Ahmad

KUCHING, Sarawak (Reuter): Malaysians call it *mayau, mao, ngau* or *miew*.

Whatever its name, the cat has always held a special place in many households.

In Kuching, capital of Malaysia's eastern state of Sarawak — and itself the Malay word for cat — they even have a museum to call their own.

Jigsaw puzzles featuring cats, wall tiles, books, stamps, decorative plates and other cat-related paraphernalia are on display in the museum on the outskirts of the city.

There are special sections on black cats, cats at play and the role of cats in Japanese and Egyptian culture in the air-conditioned museum, which does not charge an entrance fee.

Colorful posters of movies like *Cat People* and *Cat From Outer Space* are placed near pictures of famous personalities who loved cats, like author Mark Twain and British nursing pioneer Florence Nightingale.

Song albums by the top Malaysian group Alleycats are displayed alongside one by Cat Stevens.

Formerly part of the Sarawak Museum, the exhibits were transferred in 1993 to the present site on the ground floor of the Kuching North City Hall.

The special interest for cats in Kuching, a fast-growing city on Borneo island, is hardly surprising given its name.

But the history of how the city — located along the swift-flowing Sarawak River — was so named has been long forgotten.

According to local speculation, cats may have been abundant at busy ports along the Sarawak River in the past century.

Sarawak was ruled for more than a century by the so-called White Rajahs from Britain, the Brookes.

"In 1839, James Brooke (the first white Rajah) referred to the town as Kuchin', which might suggest the old word Cochin or port, as in India or Indo-China," the museum display says.

Another theory is the town derived its name in the late 19th Century from a river passing through it. The river was called Sungai Kuching as it passed near a hill covered with fruit trees known locally as Matta Kuching, literally cat's eyes (Nephelium Malaiense).

"Thus, it's settled that in 1876 the town became officially known as Kuching," the museum display says.

## Various forms

Today, the cat is as easily identified with eastern Malaysia as two other animal dwellers of the sparsely-populated rain forest state, the hornbill and the orangutan.

The cat appears in a variety of colors and forms in Kuching — as city statues, on hotel brochures and as trinkets in tourist shops.

The city's cat connection is a good selling point, said cat-lover Susie Wong, 33. "Singapore's got the lion city. I think it's unique that Kuching has the cat."

Sarawak's 25 indigenous races call it by many names, most with a strong hint of the sound the cat makes. Sarawak's majority race of Ibans calls the cat *mayau*. The Chinese call the feline *mao*, the Melanau call it *ngau*, and the Kenyah, *miew*.

The museum said Sarawak's "most sought after" breed is *nyeng*, the tabby, which is found in longhouses across the rainforest interior of the state and in villages.

"There are a lot of cat lovers in Kuching...but it's probably a coincidence," said Jacqueline Kueh, 24, who says she too is fond of the animals.

| |
|---:|
| 242,190,000 |
| 1,048,898,750 |
| 86,484,136 |
| (171,892) |
| 211,946,653 |
| 1,589,347,647 |
| 3,415,431,453 |

## CONSOLIDATED STATEMENTS OF RETAINED EARNINGS

*FOR THE YEARS ENDED*

*DECEMBER 31, 1996 AND 1995*

*(In Thousands of Rupiah)*

| | 1996 | 1995 |
|---|---:|---:|
| **RETAINED EARNINGS AT BEGINNING OF YEAR** | 211,946,653 | 128,255,533 |
| **NET INCOME** | 187,050,503 | 120,019,620 |
| **CASH DIVIDENDS** | ( 48,438,000) | ( 36,328,500 ) |
| **RETAINED EARNINGS AT END OF YEAR** | 350,559,156 | 211,946,653 |

Jakarta, April 30, 1997
PT Bakrie & Brothers

Board of Directors

ES

*Above: The Yong Tai Shop at Siniawan Bazaar is a trading post for native artefacts and antique jars from the longhouse. A Bidayuh tribesman brings in a bundle of boar tusks and monkey skulls.*

*Left: Batik artist Michael Lim paints in his studio using dyes on cotton cloth. For the past 30 years, Michael has been a full-time artist specialising in the batik media. He is famous for his paintings of orchids and birds of Sarawak, particularly the hornbill.*

# THE ART OF SARAWAK

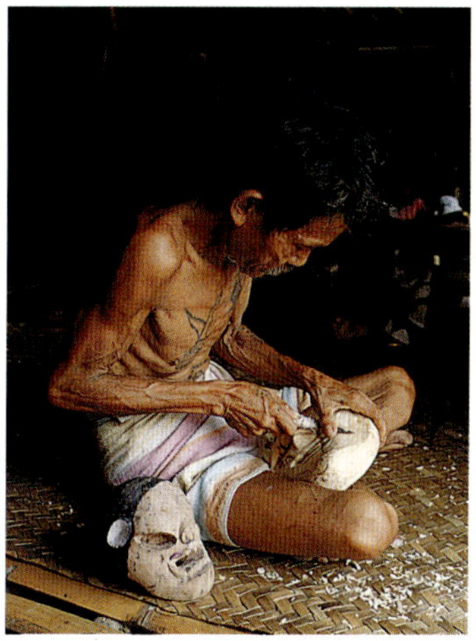

*Preceding pages: A magnificent collection of straight shafted* parang ilang *and curved* nyabur *swords.*

*Opposite: Incised bamboo tube containers of the Iban are used for keeping important documents. The smaller tubes contain the jew's-harp, a mouth musical instrument.*

*Above: An old Iban carver at work on a mask.*

The earliest evidence of art in Sarawak is found in the Great Niah Caves where paintings on the walls and pottery excavated have been carbon-dated to about 3000 B.C. Man have dwelled in these caves since 40,000 years ago.

Drum-shaped three-coloured wares and double-spouted vessels were made by the early people of Sarawak who, as they started to build shelters to live in, used the caves for burials. Wooden boat-shaped coffins discovered in the Niah Caves point to an early belief that these "spirit" boats took the dearly departed to the next world.

The term "primitive art" is very loosely used by historians and writers to describe the art of the ethnic people of Sarawak. Looking at a culture that is different and strange from our own, it is often easy to view it from a morally superior point of view and brand the unfamiliar and bizarre as "primitive" without a fuller understanding or even an attempt to understand.

Apart from a few scattered stone art like the megaliths of the Bario Highlands and the spread-eagled carved rock figurine at Santubong, stone was hardly used in any great extent for artistic expression or for building. In a tropical rainforest environment it would be only logical to use the abundance of wood for both habitat and art.

However the humid environment is very destructive to even the hardest of timber like the *belian* ironwood, not to forget the termites and other insects. The living forest quickly regains back what man has cleared, cultivated and erected. Great wooden structures such as the Melanau tall houses have succumbed to the ravages of the tropical weather and become "extinct".

Familiarity with the wood medium over the ages has resulted in its wide use by almost all the indigenous people. Hardwood is used for items meant to last for more than a lifetime, whilst the temporary would be made of softer wood.

The *klirieng*, commemorative burial poles of the Kenyah and Punan-Bah chieftains, have stood for 200 to 300 years. Iban parang or sword hilts were carved in hardwoods like *tapang* or bone.

Like in any other culture, there are objects made for daily and common use, and those made for decoration, ritual and religious purposes. The natural initial reaction is for one to be impressed with the latter rather than the former, and yet very often one finds the "humble and simple" to be the pearl of greater value. The compounded excesses in artistic expressions often cause us to turn to the essential and fundamental, which is perhaps the attraction for art collectors with regard to the art of Sarawak.

"Ethnic Art" or "Native Art" of Sarawak therefore is a term that applies to the creative expressions of the ethnic Sarawakian or the natives of Sarawak. In its pure form, one would see an item made from available local material, e.g. a wooden statue from local timber, baskets from local rattan or bamboo, all created by the hands of a Sarawakian artist or craftsman.

The idiom "No man is an island" also aptly applies to Borneo and its people. Its geographical location right in the midst of the Austronesian area has seen the movement of people over the ages of time. Sarawak's people and culture is thus, as part of Borneo, the resultant of numerous movements constrained today by the national geographical demarcations of boundaries drawn on maps.

Sarawak art may perhaps be seen as representative of Borneo art just as Sarawak is often referred to as the "Gateway to Borneo". The diversity of the culture of its more than twenty-five races coupled with the vast and varied physical environment has created a myriad of different artistic expressions.

One example is the use of the rattan fibre in making baskets and other receptacles. The difference in shapes, weaves and decoration is obvious between an Iban *lenjit* (tall sturdy harvesting basket) and the Kenyah/Penan *ajat* (expandable carry basket). The practical use or the function of the object dictates the form which usually turns out to be a beautiful time-tested response to the need, e.g. the fish-trap or *bubu*.

In contrast to the utilitarian art, the ceremonial and ritual objects are spectacular. To enter into the rustic old Iban longhouse, devoid of much decoration, spectacular in size but humble in construction and material, one is most amazed to be shown the warp-*ikat pua kumbu* or "spiritual" blankets. Technically excellent in comparison to any other *ikat* weaving of other cultures, powerful in its allegorical symbol, the *pua kumbu* is outstanding as the "high art" of the material culture of Sarawak.

The origins of the warp-*ikat* weaving technique, iron-forging, pottery, etc, have been the debate of anthropologists. Many have concluded that the Austronesian races brought them in when they migrated from the hinterland of South China through the then landmass of Sunda Shelf linking the Southeast Asian islands of today. Thus a Dong Son cultural

origin may be the ancestry of some of the indigenous people. Trade and the political powers of past history also played an important role in influencing and changing values and artistic imagery. The Chinese, Hindu, Muslim, and of recent, Christian factors have brought about immense changes in the lives of Sarawak people.

The pages following give you a glimpse into the variety of Sarawak art – native and indigenous or imported and valued as heirlooms. The multi-ethnicity and cross-cultural influences are what give the colour of Sarawak art today.

*Above: Traditional Iban clay pottery with wooden beaters that are used to emboss patterns on the surfaces of the pots.*

*Opposite: Contemporary silk warp-*ikat *weaving by artist Bangie ak Embol depicts* puchok rebong *or bamboo shoots.*

*Following pages: Fine intricate detail of a* pua kumbu *from the Betong area portrays jungle fruits and insects.*

# IBAN TEXTILES

*Pua kumbu*, the woven art of the Iban, is well known amongst textile collectors and museums because of the exquisite and intricate patterns created using the warp-*ikat* technique where patterns are tied-and-dyed on vertical threads.

Woven on a backstrap loom, these weavings played an important role in the rituals and culture of the Iban whose oral history dates back 40 generations.

The distinctive feature of Iban warp-*ikat* is the finesse employed in tieing the patterns. As the Iban weaver relates:

"The spiral curl in *pua kumbu* must be smaller than your thumb; as tight as the nail sticks to the flesh; as a tadpole adheres to a fallen leaf in the swift flowing stream; as true friendship...never betraying each other."

*Left: A fine cotton* pua kumbu *with 12 crocodiles from the Saratok district, identified by the bright colour borders. The crocodile effigy signifies the spirit of the land; thus this weaving is used during Gawai Batu, the blessing ceremony of farming implements.*

*Opposite: Detail of weaving showing Beji, an Iban hero who built a ladder to reach the heavens but fell back to earth when his ladder was eaten by termites.*

# WOVEN SYMBOLS

Designs and symbols are completely composed on the stretched out yarn, without reference to any drawings. The Iban weaver is often described as a designer (for creative expressions), a chemist (for the dyes), historian (for recording events and legends) and poet (for the poems composed to enhance each masterpiece).

Each weaver, according to her weaving status, has limitations to her expressions until she attains "master-weaver" level.

Some common symbols include birds, deer, snakes, leeches, centipedes, squirrels, frogs, flowers and fruits. The higher symbols are of humans and spirits.

*Left: A weaving recording a Gawai Burong, a festival which commemorates heroes and bravery. Four large bird effigies raised on bamboo poles celebrate the victory of young warriors in the air force.*

*Opposite: (top, left to right)*

***Symbols on the weaves***

*Crocodiles swimming amongst their prey and little spirits of the watery world;* trabai bungkok, *the war shield pattern; ritual bamboo baskets for receiving trophy skulls.*

*(bottom, left to right)*
*Wild mango motif showing the seeds inside; poison darts of the blowpipe; creepers of the jungle.*

# OF MEN AND SPIRITS

The Iban traditionally believe that life is a balance of harmonious living of men and spirits. Birds of augury and omens are carefully observed; offerings are made to appease the spirits in *miring* or sacrificial ceremonies.

Weavings with spirit images are highly regarded and rare. Many are associated with headhunting rites or the "soul-searching" trances when the shaman goes on a spiritual journey to heal a sick person.

*Opposite, left: An unusual weaving depicting the Spirits of the Air; some emphasised in blue (indigo dye).*

*Opposite, right: Three decorated war heroes named Bujang Mali.*

*Right:* Engkaramba *or Spirits of Headhunting, depicted with hands carrying trophy skulls. The sex of the spirit figure is denoted by the symbol between the lower limbs.*

# IBAN JACKETS AND SKIRTS

Special jackets or *kalambi* are woven for use by the shaman as protective coverings. They are full of the *Engkaramba* spirit figures imbued with power for the rituals and religious duties to be performed. Mostly woven in the warp-*ikat* technique, some are embellished with a patch of *songket* of supplementary weft weaving, or a detail trim of tapestry weaving, usually located at the back tail portion of the jacket.

*Left: A long jacket of a powerful* lemambang *bard and shaman. Repeated motifs depict the multi-limbed spirit. The bottom patch is the* songket *which shows four anthropomorphic figures.*

*Above, top and bottom: Jackets with magical motifs –* Engkaramba *spirit figures and the auspicious bird motifs or* baju burong.

*Opposite: Six short* kain kebat *or tube-skirts with fine details. Only minor creatures are depicted in skirts, e.g. leeches (symbol of fertility); shrews, flowers, creepers, barking deer; eagles.*

# MAGICAL JACKETS

The folklore of the Orang Ulu people carries many stories of how their heroes and warriors have been imbued with supernatural power by adorning special jackets made from the pelts of clouded leopards and bears. Some of these were embellished with hornbill feathers and pangolin scales. A jacket with hornbill feathers denotes a great fighter who has taken part in successful expeditions.

*Left: This rare crocodile jacket, once used in ancient rituals, belonged to a female shaman.*

*Below: Tiny polished cowrie shells were used as currency in the old barter trade days. These shells were carefully embroidered onto the handwoven cotton tube-skirt, forming geometric patterns.*

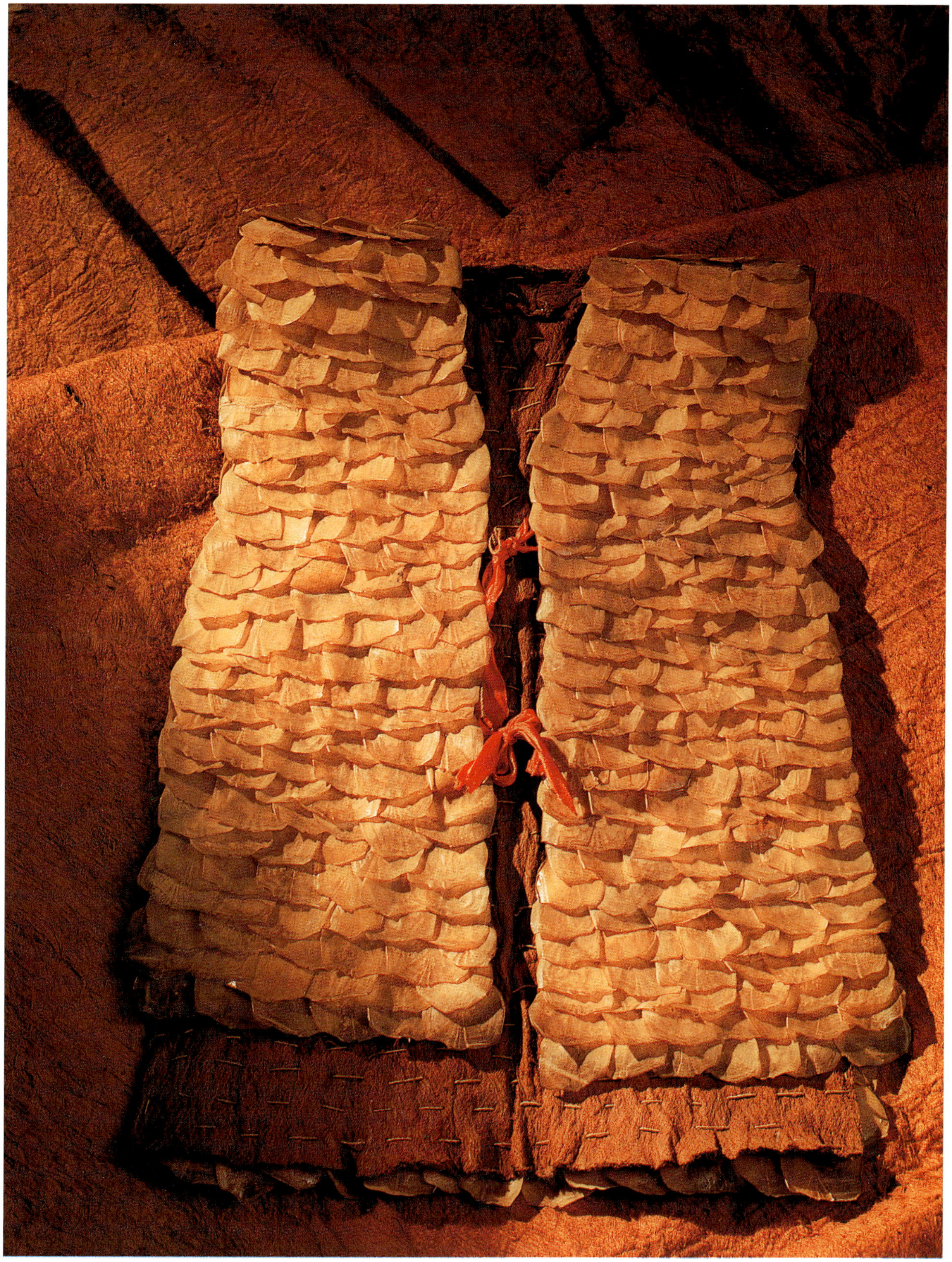

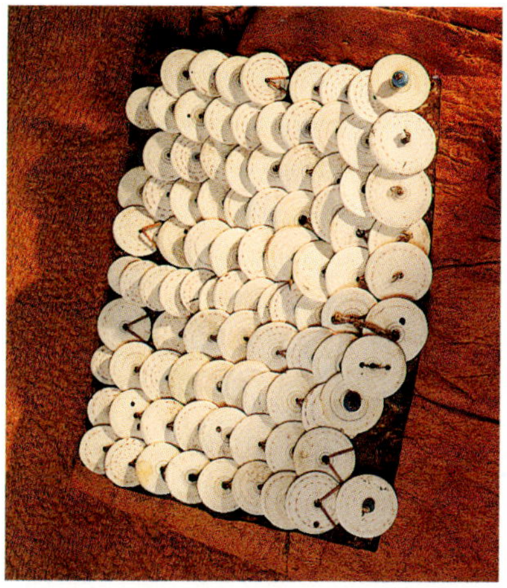

*Left: The pangolin or anteater is hunted for its medicinal value. Its scales add magical power to the shaman's jacket.*

*Above, top: Polished and ground into discs, the giant clamshells act as a protective armour for this warrior's jacket.*

*Above, bottom: A Kenyah warrior's animal-hide jacket is covered at the back with hornbill feathers, enhancing the agility and prowess of his movements in the jungle.*

*Opposite: A rhinoceros hornbill's head decorates a Kenyah chieftain's skullcap which is embellished with cowrie shell beads.*

*Left, top: A Dusun aristocratic lady's hat of rattan basketry is covered with cowrie shells traded with the lowland tribes.*

*Left, bottom: Two Lun Bawang hats of wickerwork are decorated with small cowrie shells. The tops are capped with brass (at left) and red glass beads (on the right).*

*Below: Melanau treasure boxes made of rattan frames and sago palm bast (at left) and* bemban *reed basketry (on the right).*

## ORANG ULU HATS AND CRAFTS

Living in the interior parts and highlands the Orang Ulu make use of various bark fibres for cloth, and palm leaves, rattan and other jungle reeds for creating hats, boxes and other containers. The art of embellishment is highly decorative: beads of cowrie shells, porcelain buttons and ancient glass beads are arranged to form interesting patterns and textures.

# ETHNIC HATS

Various types of hats are made from the dried leaves of *nipah* and fan palms. Most hats are conical and large, although the Orang Ulu make a round, flat brimmed sunhat. Ceremonial hats are more decorative and colourful compared to functional ones.

Elaborate beaded panels, patchwork and rosettes decorate the Orang Ulu ceremonial hat. The Iban women specially weave motifs of birds, fish and ferns out of split bamboo to enhance their farm hats.

The popular Melanau *terendak* conical hat is overlaid with painted *nipah* leaves in geometric design.

*Opposite: A large Melanau ceremonial hat (30" in diameter) is made of large dried palm leaves while the foliate scroll decorations on the hat are of cut-out palm leaves.*

*Top left: A Melanau shaman's hat is decorated with spirit figures.*

*Top right: An Orang Ulu sunhat has central beaded decoration.*

*Right: Hats of a Bidayuh priestess with interwoven orchid fibres and painted dragon blood patterns.*

# ORANG ULU BEADWORK

Beadwork among the Orang Ulu tribes, such as the Kayan, Kenyah and Kelabit, are used to decorate the simple tunic jackets and tube-skirts of bark cloth or plain cotton. Tiny multicoloured glass seed beads were barter trade items that originated from Italy, Bohemia, England, and other European glass centres. Patterns are carefully drawn out before stringing begins.

*Above: The* aso *or dragon-dog motif on this jacket is a symbol used only for aristocratic families.*

*Top right: The central panel on this tube-skirt has a seed-beaded* aso *motif, with borders of cowrie shells.*

*Centre and bottom right: Two examples of skirts with the spread-eagle humanoid motifs reserved for use by upper class women.*

# BABY CARRIERS

The Kayan and Kenyah traditionally carry their babies in rattan back-carriers with wooden bottoms. These carriers are elaborately decorated with multicoloured beaded panels of spread-eagled spirit figures, *naga* (dragon) masks, leopards and hornbills. Ancient glass beads and amulets of bear-claws or leopard's fangs add to the spiritual protection of the baby carried within.

*Above, top and bottom: Only babies of aristocratic families may have carriers with the full-figure motif. The curled tendril-like motif is characteristic of Kayan/Kenyah art. The central human figures are intertwined with the hornbill head motif.*

*Left: A special baby carrier with beaded masks motif and three rows of leopard's fangs.*

# ORANG ULU JEWELLERY

Among the Sarawak people, the Orang Ulu is probably the most closely related to the mainland Asiatic races. This is evident in the brass earrings and eardrops worn by women around their stretched earlobes. Metal forging and smithing was a well-known skill of the Kayan and Kenyah, although another group, the Malohs, are well known as brass workers and silversmiths.

Bracelets were made of ivory, wood, silver and brass coiled over rattan rings and fern-stems. The early beadwork waist belts and skull caps were fashioned from large and heavy semi-precious stones like cornelian, agate and clamshells. Later types feature smaller decorative glass beads. Early Orang Ulu jewellery was basic and simple.

*Right (upper left): Earrings were solid brass rings or fruit-shaped brass drops with a small gap to pass between stretched earlobes. (Upper right): An unusual solid brass neck-plate is formed by fusing together brass coils. (Centre): Simple circular cut sections of ivory are incised with pattern to make bracelets or strung together for armlets. (Bottom left): Bast-fibre round loops are enhanced with tiny silver and brass rings to form men's leg bands. (Bottom right): Hand-polished shell and cornelian stone beads are strung into waist belts.*

*Above: Orang Ulu jewellery. The* aso *or dragon-dog motif was cast in brass for earrings (centre and bottom right) and carved out of hornbill ivory (left). A hairpin with a boar tusk combined with* aso *woodcarving is unusual (top right).*

*Far left: Arm bracelets were carved out of the giant clamshell while the necklaces are cowrie shells.*

*Left: Brass bells and shells were combined with boar tusks into a shaman's necklace.*

# BIDAYUH JEWELLERY

Ceremonial jewellery for Bidayuh chieftains and shamans comprises elaborate necklaces of large, old coloured glass beads strung with animal teeth and claws, interspersed with brass bells "to keep the antique beads from fighting." Some of these old beads are used in "child-naming" ceremonies and are believed to have supernatural powers, particularly useful when dealing with evil spirits.

Each of the Bidayuh subtribes, like the Jagoi, Bukar-Sadong, Biatah and Selakau, has its own distinguishing bead jewellery.

*Left: Ketua Gawai or Ceremonial Chief's necklace consists of chunky translucent green, blue and amber glass beads, brass bells and bear claws.*

*Above: Bidayuh Bukar-Sadong man's collar necklace of leopard fangs and bear claws are combined with shell and beads.*

*Left: Tiara headdress, silver combs, necklaces and silver button-necklace.* (Datin Paduka Empiang Jabu Collection)

*Right: Silver coiled* rawai *corsets (top right) and bracelets (bottom right) are of native Maloh craftsmanship. Other knitted silver belts with large repousse buckles (bottom centre), coin belts and powder boxes (centre and top left) were made by Chinese silversmiths specially for the Iban market.*

# IBAN JEWELLERY

The festive costume of the Iban woman would be incomplete without the resplendent display of her family heirloom silver. From her tiara headdress (*sugu tinggi*) to her anklets, her total silver accessories could weigh several kilograms. Past official reports recorded river accidents where maidens have drowned, weighed down by their silver *rawai* corsets and belts of silver dollar coins.

The *rawai* is a close-fitting corset composed of a series of cane hoops covered with tiny silver pinned together with brass wire. It functions both as costume and jewellery.

# IBAN CEREMONIAL ORNAMENTS

The Iban man's ceremonial attire, consisting of a six-metre long red loincloth and the *kalambi* jacket, is incomplete without the feathered headdress and the *pedang kerajaan*, ceremonial sword decorated with hornbill feathers. The swords are either original "Rajah Brooke" era or Colonial copies with handcrafted silverwork added to the shafts. To secure the ceremonial sword around the waist, a belt is used made of plaited hemp. Dangling adjacent to the sword is an ornament featuring a rhinoceros hornbill casque with tassles of tiny glass beads and brass bells.

*Opposite: Beaded ornamental belt attachment with a hornbill casque is worn as a talisman by Iban chiefs.*

*Above: The ceremonial sword of Tan Sri Datuk Amar Alfred Jabu, Deputy Chief Minister.*

# ORANG ULU TATTOO PATTERN

The art of tattooing is highly developed among the Orang Ulu and Iban people. The Orang Ulu, particularly the Kenyah women of aristocratic status, are finely tattooed on their arms, fingers, feet and thighs. Some Iban men, besides having tattoos on the arms, legs and torso have tattoos on the throat as a symbol of bravery. Designs are first incised on a wooden block and printed on the skin to be finely pricked with needle and dye.

*Above: The tattoo needle and blotter are finely carved as are the bird-shaped dye bowl and box for keeping all the tattoo implements.*

*Right: A collection of tattoo blocks for a Kenyah woman's arms and thighs.*

# HUDOK MASK AND HORNBILL CARVINGS

*Hudok* masks are used by the Kayan and Kenyah Orang Ulu in rituals associated with the planting of padi, in healing ceremonies or for merrymaking at festivals.

Donning the mask, the *hudok* dancer scares away evil spirits from the longhouse. By clowning around, the dancer provokes tears of laughter which is believed to help water newly planted padi.

Elaborate carved effigies of the *Kenyalang* hornbill bird, a symbolic representation of the Iban God of War, Sengalang Burong, are made during celebrations of Gawai Burong festivals. The effigies, used to invoke blessings upon warriors during the ancient headhunting days, are now used to commemorate those Iban heroes in the army, air force or navy.

*Left:* Hudok neng *Kayan mask with the typical large eyes, exposed teeth and exaggerated long pierced ears with eardrops and woven basket cap.*

*Right:* Kenyalang *effigies from different Iban regions display artistic variations in composition.*

*Opposite: A collection of carved deer horn bodkins.*

*Left: Carved shuttles with foliate scroll designs are usually of light softwood.*

*Right: Coconut shell measures for dye-bath mordants and oils are incised with patterns of ferns and flowers.*

*Below: The beaters are usually shaped like swords with carved handles of motifs of plants or birds and animals.*

# WEAVING IMPLEMENTS

The finesse of Iban carving is best expressed in the wooden shuttles, beaters, coconut shell measures, horn bodkins and spinning wheels made by the Iban men for their womenfolk, who are weavers. Such beautiful implements usually add prestige and status to the accomplished "master-weaver", inspire her creativity and lend protection or spiritual covering over the *pua kumbu* weaving that she is working on.

# WOODEN BUCKLES

Planting and harvesting padi are major activities in the life of the peoples of Sarawak. Among the Iban and related groups, very finely woven baskets are made by the womenfolk themselves. The harvest basket is worn around the waist with a rattan band attached by a finely carved wooden buckle made by the men.

*Above: Buckle designs vary from the ornate foliate scroll incorporating a hornbill motif (bottom left) to the sculptural bird or water-snail (bottom right). Each has a catch that will fasten to the rattan loop on the basket rim (top left).*

*Left: (clockwise from right) Naive-like buckles of a pig, deer, snail, tortoise and eagle.*

# CARVED BOWLS

Among the Orang Ulu, the Berawan Kayan and Kenyah tribes were reputed artists in wood. Carved bowls and spoons, especially those with humanoid and spirit figures, were made for pagan rituals and offerings. Today, these items are produced for the art and souvenir market instead for many of the Berawan Kayan and Kenyah have become Christians.

*Left: A round carved wooden bowl (made from the* tapang *or* koompassia excelsa *tree) with deer horn decoration on the rim and two decorative carved spoons.*

*Above: Old carved wooden offering bowls with spirit figures.*

# CARVED DOORS

Among the Kayan and Kenyah, doorways to the individual *bilik* or rooms of the chiefs and aristocratic families were enhanced with carvings and paintings, both to denote status as well as to repel malevolent spirits.

Large slabs of the buttress roots of the *tapang* tree measuring three to four feet wide are usually cut for these doors; occasionally the *belian* ironwood is also used.

*Left: An important chief's door collected by Charles Hose in the 1890s is carved from a two-inch thick solid* tapang *wood (koompassia excelsa). The door, studded with circular inlay shells, depicts a* naga *(dragon) with a protective spirit at the top.*

*Opposite: Two other doors from the Hose Collection depict the victory of the protective spirit over evil (right) and other guardian spirits (left).*

## MASKS

Made of softwood, and stained black with soot or white with lime, these masks were not made for any ritual purposes, but function as *indai guru* ("mother teacher"). Kept in the *sadau* or attic of the family apartments, the masks were worn only on certain occasions, to deter children from naughty deeds.

*Left: Two antique masks typically showing exposed teeth and eyes.*

*Opposite: There is no hard and fast rule in the design of the expressions on the masks. Masks are often carved in human likeness.*

# WOODCARVING

Woodcarving was generally a man's domain in artistic expression, be it in making small objects like smoking pipes, spoons and *tuntun* pig-charm sticks, or the large, life-size statues and the huge *klirieng* (burial poles) of the Orang Ulu.

The carvings reflect not only the creative talents but also the spiritual traditions of the artist. The carver carefully selects the wood he would work on. For large pieces, which require a tree to be felled, special offerings to appease the spirit of the jungle are made.

The carver's tools are rather basic: an adze, axe and an assortment of penknives. For fine work and polishing, certain types of jungle leaves are used.

*Left: Iban* tuntun *pig-charm sticks were used as measures for the height of the traps. The crouched humanoid spirit figures, carved at the top of the hardwood stick, is believed to have magical powers to lure the wild boars to the trap.*

*Right: Two important Kenyah statues carved for the Peace-Keeping Ceremony at Marudi, Baram River in 1898. Now housed in the Sarawak Museum they have over the years become symbols of virility.*

# MELANAU CARVING

Among the animistic Melanau people, the practice of their religion, Liko, also involves the belief of healing by making effigies of the "sickness" spirits to be cast out from the sick person. These spirits are closely related to the environment, being of "air", "water" or "land", and are usually depicted in a sitting or crouching posture.

During the healing ceremony, as many as a dozen different *belum* effigies are arranged in a model boat called *rabung*. This spirit boat is then cast out to sea at the completion of the ceremony.

Many Melanau are fishermen; special carved light wood or bone fishing fetishes are attached to the nets to ensure a bountiful catch.

*Above: Painted softwood* belum *sickness effigies are "activated" when their eyes are pierced or "opened".*

*Right: Carved bone fishing fetishes with the characteristic crouching postures of the spirit figure.*

# GUARDIAN FIGURES

Life-size ancestral figures and guardian statues were carved in human likeness by many Bornean interior people such as the Bidayuh. Often found at the junctions of footpaths leading to their villages and longhouses, they protect against evil spirits. Exposed to the tropical weather, even the hardest of wood like *belian* ironwood show signs of wear and tear. Combined with algae and fungus growth, these *tigundu* figures exude a mystical and fascinating charm.

A curious monkey figure (left) serves as a stool. Others depict obese male slaves (below right) and female slaves as bases. The clouded leopard (bottom) is a much revered animal. Its fangs also decorate the chieftain's pierced ears.

# WOOD FURNITURE

In the longhouses and village homes, people sat on mats on the floor. Among the Kayan and Kenyah of the Belaga area , the chiefs had special stools carved for them. Like throne-chairs, they denote the chief's authority and position. Carved out of solid chunks of medium hardwood, they are heavy and sturdy. Another ethnic group, the Berawan of the Tinjar river, were well-known carvers who made impressive tables from large slabs cut from the buttress roots of the *tapang* tree.

*Above: The four corners of this huge table are supported by* naga *or dragons. Large old table pieces were used as table platforms for the chiefs, although more recent pieces were made specifically as house furniture.*

*Right: A crouching figure of a dog is used as a corner support for a solid ironwood table.*

*Opposite: Very fine black and natural mats and carry baskets are made by the nomadic Penan and the Kayan/Kenyah. The black colour is achieved by soaking the split rattan in a bath of mud, leaves and roots. The decorative motifs created include ferns, fruits, creepers and shoots, leeches, snakes and birds.*

*Left, top: Bidayuh baskets for daily use are plain and robustly made of rattan. Below, bottom: For ceremonial use they are finely worked with patterns of creepers and fruits or combined with strips of dried, wild orchid stems.*

*Left, bottom: Kelabit and Lun Bawang highland people make very sturdy carry baskets. A soft strap of plaited palm or a strap cloth acts as a head strap fastened to loops on the baskets.*

*Below, top: A collection of Iban harvesting baskets. The ripe padi is cut and collected into the squat baskets fastened round the waist, before being deposited inside the tall lenjit basket to be carried back to the longhouse.*

*Following pages: Iban seed baskets bear similar design to the tendril or hook motifs in their cotton weavings. The dark red colour known as "dragon's blood" is obtained from boiling rattan seeds.*

# BASKETS

The weaving and plaiting of an abundance of jungle creepers and fibres into baskets and mats is common to all indigenous Sarawakians. The robust and pliable rattan or cane is widely used. Other palm fronds as well as pandanus leaves, orchid stems and tree bark can all be combined or separately woven into containers.

As the daily life of the people rotates around the planting and harvesting of padi or rice, baskets are made for storing the padi seeds; special ones for the rituals before sowing; others for sowing, harvesting, gathering of jungle vegetables, and as fish-traps.

# POTTERY

Ceramics have been traded from China as early as the 9th to 10th centuries. Glazed stoneware storage jars called *tempayan,* in hues of brown to green and blue with embossed and incised patterns, are greatly valued heirlooms and symbols of wealth. Rare pieces were greatly revered and some were associated with legends and supernatural powers. The recurrent decorations on these jars are dragons and floral scrolls.

*Opposite, top: Family heirloom* tempayan *jars line the walls of an Iban longhouse room. More ordinary ones would be used for storing* tuak *(rice wine).*

*Opposite, bottom: A collection of rare green and blue-glazed Chinese jars from the Sarawak Museum.*

*Left: Valuable Swatow Ming and 19th-century Dutch Delft large plates are protected with rattan cases and hung near the cooking hearth of a longhouse.*

## BRASS CANNONS AND GONGS

The art of metal-casting was known in the Brunei Sultanate as long ago as the 16th century. Early trade with China, India and the Middle East may have ushered in the craft along with the forms and decorative motifs.

Brass cannons were collected by the people as a status symbol of power, wealth and influence. The large plain ones, *bedil buloh,* were real weapons; the more decorative pieces like the *bedil naga* with designs of *naga* (dragons) and crocodiles were ceremonial and heirloom items.

Miniature brass cannons were made as a form of currency, as an exchange of gifts symbolising diplomatic ties or merely as a whimsical expression of art.

*Above: The crocodile form (at top) reflects the strength and power of the reptile – common in Sarawak – as well as its legendary aura. Single-barrel, double-barrel cannons were also made. The buffalo-shaped piece (at bottom) is rare.*

*Right: Highly treasured dragon-shaped cannons.*

*Opposite: Gongs with embossed* naga *serve as beautiful status symbols as well as musical instruments.*

# KETTLES

Metal, as a durable element, is a highly regarded material, playing an important part in the culture of Sarawak people. Among the Orang Ulu and Iban people, a newly married couple would be seated on a large gong to be blessed with longevity, fertility and spiritual strengthening.

Brassware was valued and treasured by all tribes as currency, often used as traditional payments for fines. Large ornate kettles and other containers played significant roles in ceremonies and rituals.

*Left: Early Brunei brass kettles such as this display a more naive expression of figures like horses, cattle and other mythical animals.*

*Top: The later pieces with Chinese style dragons and frogs on the sides and a fu-dog type animal on the lid appear to be influenced by Chinese ceramics.*

*Bottom: The covered container bears more similarity to traditional Malay lacquerware.*

*Opposite: Various sizes of rectangular boxes ornately embellished with foliate scrolls and geometrical designs reflect the Muslim origin of the* tepak sirih.

# BETEL BOXES AND CONTAINERS

Betel-nut (*sirih*) chewing was a common social practice among the peoples of Borneo. To offer *sirih* to visitors was an important gesture of welcome and acceptance into the family or community.

Chewing betel nut has long been known in the Malay/Indonesian Archipelago, although the practice may have originated from India and spread through the trade routes.

The ingredients for making the *sirih* are: betel leaves (from the piper betel vine), areca nut (*pinang*), gambier, tobacco and lime. These are kept in small covered brass containers within a special box or an open receptacle. A special areca-nut cutter and slicer completes the *tepak sirih* set.

*Top: A large, heavy heirloom container tells a legend of the naga and the hunter.*

*Centre: A buffalo container combines an oil lamp with sirih box.*

*Bottom: A bird-shaped open receptable has several brass containers for the lime, tobacco and a special open fretwork holder for the betel leaves.*

*Right and opposite: Stripes and plaids are interwoven with golden threaded motifs. Each* kain songket *skirt or* sarong *has a feature panel which usually includes a* pucuk *or plant shoot, as seen in the triangular motif on this page (at bottom right) and on the opposite page (bottom right).*

## MALAY TEXTILES

Known as *kain songket*, this handwoven textile of gold and silver threads combined with fine cotton or silk yarn is a legacy passed down from the Brunei Sultanate days. As their religion frowns upon the depiction of images, Malay weavers chose geometric patterns of flowers, rosettes, stars and stripes for their design. Early weavings were of natural dyes from turmeric (orange, yellow) and bark (maroon), until commercial coloured yarn were available. Worn only on auspicious occasions, such as weddings, *kain songket* was the attire for the aristocracy, "the *perabangan*".

# MALAY JEWELLERY

Given the prohibition on human representations or figurines, design motifs used in Malay jewellery such as its necklaces and buckles are usually of flowers and fruits. Sometimes precious stones like rubies and emeralds traded from India were added, as well as locally mined diamonds from Kalimantan Borneo. Many of the traditional goldsmiths are Brunei Malay, Kalimantan Malay or Maloh people.

*Opposite:* A rantai-papan *gold necklace features a central pendant with a ruby stone; of Indonesian Malay design its Manorah motif shows Hindu influence.*

*Above: A gold gilded necklace with the* Bunga cempaka, *a scented flower motif.*

*Left: Golden buckle with rosette motif similar to the woven* kain songket.

# PERANAKAN JEWELLERY

Having settled in Sarawak, the Chinese over the generations intermarried and became known as Peranakan Chinese. They brought with them their skills in gold and silver smithing.

The nyonya (Peranakan ladies) wore their hair in a small bun and use various types of gold hairpins, some studded with diamonds, pearls and jade. They dressed like the Malay ladies, wearing a long-sleeved tunic dress held together in front with big brooches or *kerongsang*, the latter beautifully crafted in silver or gold and set with precious stones.

*Above: Butterfly and bird hairpins of jade and natural pearls are set in gold.*

*Left: A bee, cicada, bird, spider and butterfly brooches are worn by wealthy nyonya ladies.*

*Opposite: Gold brooches with diamonds are sometimes converted into pendants. Necklaces of such floral design were also popular with Malays.*

# THE ARCHITECTURAL DIMENSION — TRADITIONS

*Preceding pages: Man in harmony with nature. An Orang Ulu longhouse sits amidst the grandeur of an immense forest behind the Sarawak Cultural Village.*

*Opposite: The Melanau Rumah Tinggi or "Tall House" is a spacious three-storey wood and attap house with solid tree trunks as posts.*

*Above: Every longhouse community has guardian figures to ward off evil spirits.*

"No man is an island" – the traditional way of living in Sarawak has always been communal, whether it be in longhouses or in the kampongs or villages. The phenomenon of "safety in number" is very much part of the traditional society, particularly in times of inter-tribal hostility and the need for survival in a difficult environment.

The most basic of jungle shelters would be the makeshift huts of the nomadic Penan: a few sturdy wooden posts tied together with rattan, and palm thatch for covering, all quickly put together, is quite adequate protection from the rain for a few days or weeks before they journey on.

From such basic forms to the development of the longhouse, one can quickly note that the building material remains the same – wood and thatch, although the buildings are progressively larger and made more sturdy for a longer lifespan.

The majority of Sarawak's peoples today live in rural communities. Of the main ethnic groups, the Iban, Bidayuh and Orang Ulu traditionally build longhouses although some settlements today consist of single-family dwellings. The Malay and Melanau live in separate houses in a kampong, while the Chinese build simple farmhouses or live in two-storey shophouses, a convenient way of combining family and business life.

The longhouse is the oldest architectural form in Sarawak, going as far back as the history of the ethnic groups can be remembered. Among the Iban, Bidayuh and Orang Ulu, the basic concept of the longhouse is similar. It is a linear arrangement under one common roof of separate apartments, the doors of which open out to a common hall or gallery:

> From this corridor there is often only a single exit; in any case one main exit. This main door, through which everything entering or existing must pass, is very important. The evil spirits must be prevented from passing through. Threatening faces are carved into the door, often accompanied by the stylised *aso* motifs. (*Ave* 1981:96)

The above description applies to the the Kayan and Kenyah longhouses. In the Iban longhouse, the threatening figure or face is carved into the notched staircase usually made of ironwood. Amongst the Bidayuh, carved statues (*tigundu*) are strategically placed at the approach to the longhouse near a reception point. There are similarities in the spiritual beliefs of all the Bornean

*Above, top and bottom: The Bidayuh village of Kampong Seratau in the Serian District group their rice granaries away from their longhouse for fire-safety reasons. The granaries, little thatched huts on stilts with circular wooden plate capitals – an anti-rodent device – have each a drying platform of split bamboo.*

*Opposite: In the weaving longhouse of Rumah Atong in Sungai Kain, the Iban women give their collection of* pua kumbu *warp-ikat weaving an airing once in a while to prevent mildew and roach damage.*

peoples, and the creation of a village was an important ritual act:

> Taking possession of previously uncultivated land, organising the clearing of the bush, that synonym of chaos, was equivalent to repeating the creation of the universe. That is why the village was of such importance to its people. Their first sacrifices were to the earth spirits, who owned the land. The founders of the new village took some stones from the "mother village" to the place of sacrifice which thereby became the germ of the "daughter village" which was also a concrete expression of a lasting privileged relationship between the two villages. This relationship is extended all the way back to the mythical original village of the people. This first village, the gift of the gods to the original ancestors, is the archetype and the model for all the villages of a tribe. (*Stohr*, 1981:11)

There are therefore strict ritual prohibitions that have to be adhered to in the building of a longhouse, and in building new family apartments.

Sited usually near a river or stream because of the availability of water supply, fishing and ease of transportation, and on high ground for strategic defence purposes, each longhouse varies in size from about twenty to over eighty apartments. Sometimes, because of site constraints two parallel longhouses are constructed as the community grows. The average house may accommodate between two to three hundred people. Larger longhouses have between seven to eight hundred people. The mere size of the building is impressive, and the hive of activity in the common gallery or verandah can be overwhelming: adults' chatter, children running about along the timber flooring, dogs barking. As the longhouse is raised on wooden stilts or piles at least a full storey above the ground, the area below is where the pigs and chickens are kept, foraging around for whatever rubbish or food that is thrown down from the family kitchens above.

The Iban and Orang Ulu build more solid longhouses that are habitable for several generations. The well-known houses have impressive solid ironwood columns and large hand-hewn floor boards. Longhouses are broken up or removed either because of natural disasters like fires or epidemics or for superstitious reasons, but most commonly because the soil

of the surrounding area has been worked out.

Bidayuh longhouses tend to be built of less durable material because the areas around them have fewer of the big trees for lumber. Their construction makes use of a lot of bamboo for which they have developed methods of preservation for a longer lifespan.

Just as there are strict rituals involved in the construction of a longhouse, there are many spiritual observances in the felling of trees or gathering of jungle produce. Before chopping down a huge tree for lumber, the Iban would place a blowpipe at its base and make food offerings on a piece of *pua kumbu* textile to appease the Spirit of the Tree. Bidayuh people would give notice to the spirits of trees and make sacrifics to them.

Superstitions die hard, and local people still take no chances in offending the spirits whether good or evil. In any construction site today, whether it be the building of an Iban, Orang Ulu, Chinese or Malay house, special prayers are said and offerings made. Contractors of large commercial developments in the towns erect little red "spirit houses" to appease the spirits of the land to safeguard their works. The spirit world is very real to Sarawakians. Christians hold "house-blessing"; Muslims have special prayers for their new homes called *doa selamat*, and the animists still hang their special charms and amulets to ward off the evil spirits.

# THE BIDAYUH LONGHOUSE

The Bidayuh longhouse is traditionally built on stilts using round tree-trunks as posts and beams. Raised at least three metres from the ground, the floor of the gallery and open platform is made of bamboo trunks which have been split in half. The roof and end walls of the longhouse are covered with palm thatch. To allow ventilation and daylight into the otherwise rather dark interior of the family rooms, a flap is made in the roof, kept open by a rattan rope which is secured to a post. In the same way the main door is kept shut by a similar pulley system consisting of a rattan rope and a heavy stone weight used as a closing device.

*Left: The* tanju *or open deck of the longhouse is useful for drying padi and other crops. It is linked to the* baruk *or headhouse in the background.*

*Right: The communal gallery space is a cool shaded verandah where activities such as the threshing and pounding of rice (in the foreground) and craft-making take place.*

*Left: Apartments are often interconnected by doorways, especially when families are kin-related. The family hearth is usually built within the family rooms although a smaller fireplace may be found on the gallery where the pounding of padi takes place. The loft, besides being a store, is also used as sleeping quarters for the young women.*

# THE BIDAYUH HEADHOUSE

*Above: In the* baruk*, a Bidayuh lady tends to the central fireplace while village elders hold discussions on a raised platform.*

The most outstanding feature of the Bidayuh longhouse architecture is the headhouse or *baruk*. The *baruk* has survived as the centre of the community. In the centre of the hall the old skulls of the headhunting days are placed in reverence above the fireplace. Here, the village chief and elders discuss local politics and community issues with the people; festivals are celebrated and ceremonies are conducted by the shamans. In the past, war drums and gongs were kept at the headhouse. Today they are used for festivals and ceremonies.

The floor is constructed of a double layer of split bamboo, for structural stability and to prevent attacks by enemy spears from below. A raised timber platform around the inside perimeter acts as a seating and sleeping area for the young bachelors of the village. The conical roof of overlapping palm thatch has open skylights at the lower sections, allowing in light and fresh air to circulate. The whole structure is supported by an elaborate framing system devised by using selected lengths of a local timber, which are tied together with rattan and ropes made from tree bark.

# THE TRADITIONAL IBAN LONGHOUSE

The traditional Iban longhouse is smaller than the contemporary model. Each family room is about four metres wide while the cooking hearth is located near the door to the common gallery or *ruai*. Walls are made of tree bark, the flooring is split palm trunk, and the roof is palm thatch or ironwood shingles.

Oriented to face north/south, Iban longhouses are built on high ground along the riverbanks, the height of the stilts depending on the terrain. The formal entrance to the longhouse is always at the eastern or western end.

*Left: The bark of the* meranti *tree (shorea) is a hardy exterior wall for this old longhouse at the Cultural Village.*

*Above: Rumah Along at Nanga Sumpa has a sidewall and roof of corrugated iron sheets, first introduced over forty years ago.*

*Every family maintains their bilik (private apartment) and ruai (communal gallery) as well as the tanju (open deck) segment of their longhouse. Drying padi and weaving (left) are daily chores seen at Rumah Along (below).*

*Left: The communal gallery space is decorated with dried palm fronds for a Gawai festival. Woven* pua kumbu *are wrapped around farming implements that would be used in a blessing ceremony.*

*Above, top: An Iban woman sits on a wooden stool to cook* kueh jala *or rice cookies. A notched log serves as a staircase leading from the family apartment to the attic.*

*Above, bottom: Woven rattan knot detail on crossbeams.*

# THE CONTEMPORARY IBAN LONGHOUSE

As the Iban communities became more settled and prosperous over the years, villagers built larger longhouses using more durable material. Support posts of ironwood and large hardwood floor boards are not uncommon.

The gallery has been enlarged and family apartments have been widened to provide more space for the extended family. A separate annex is also created. Living space, which is now larger than in the traditional longhouse, is filled with household furniture such as cupboards and cabinets, three-piece suites and coffee tables, purchased in the Chinese bazaars. Individuality and personal taste are manifested in the treatment of the *bilik* wall facing the *ruai* with carefully incised woodcarving, bas-relief panelling, or coloured paintwork.

*Right: The living room has a wooden settee for private family reception with stairs leading to the attic area. The door in the background leads to the common gallery.*

*Far left: In the* sadau *or attic area, mosquito nets designate individual sleeping space.*

*Left: Carved grillework of* belian *ironwood and casement windows allow for cross-ventilation in the attic.*

*Below: Prized pieces of* pua kumbu *decorate the* communal *gallery walls on special festival days. An Iban woman weaves the* pua songket *on a portable backstrap loom.*

*Right: In the more remote Pelagus River, the Iban longhouse is built a full double-storey raised on stilts. Walls are timber weatherboards split by chainsaw by the owners. The building of a longhouse is a communal effort.*

*Above: On an ordinary day, only women, children and the older folk are in the longhouse as the men are at work in the timber camps or the towns. When not working in the rice-fields, the women are busy making hats, baskets and mats.*

*Left: An old man mending his fishing net.*

# THE ORANG ULU LONGHOUSE

The Kenyah and Kayan aristocracies are traditionally known for building impressive longhouses. This is expressed in their larger and grander apartments with high roofs as symbols of their status and superiority. The chief's verandah is also wider to allow more room for his subjects to gather. His apartment walls are painted with decorative symbols of his status: human heads, human figures, tigers and birds.

Many contemporary Orang Ulu longhouses are composed of two separate parallel blocks. The first is a separate kitchen block which consists of a series of hearths which are linked to the corresponding family apartments in the second block by a covered passage. The second two-storey block consists of family apartments on the upper level and a gallery on the lower storey. Examples of such longhouses can be found at Ulong Palang and Pa' Ukat in the Kelabit Highlands and Uma Nyaveng and Uma Juman on the Balui River.

Most Orang Ulu longhouses are now kept very neat and clean. Like the Bidayuh, the Orang Ulu have separate rice barns set away from the longhouse. Pigs are not left to wander all over the compound, nor are dogs found all over the verandah.

*Left: The chief's unit in this Orang Ulu longhouse at the Sarawak Cultural Village is decorated with the "Tree of Life" painting on the wooden wall. A fireplace lies below the trophy skulls from headhunting days.*

## THE MELANAU RUMAH TINGGI

The old traditional dwelling of the Melanau people was a Rumah Tinggi ("Tall House"). It was similar to the longhouse except that it was raised about six metres higher and was about three storeys high. As a security measure against attacks from pirates and enemies, the Melanau built their house in such a way that they could draw up their notched steps at night. The flooring, which consisted of a double layer of palm trunks, allowed for ventilation but was impenetrable to spears. The family apartments were also at a higher level. At the third level, the valuable possessions of the family were stored.

*Opposite: The Rumah Tinggi at the scenic Sarawak Cultural Village is reconstructed from museum records. Above: In a corner of the common gallery, a Melanau shaman performs a healing ceremony. Notched stairs leads to the family apartments. Left: Inside the apartments there are smaller cubicle-like bedrooms. Family heirlooms of brass-ware line the wide corridor area where a notched trunk stairs lead to the third storey.*

# MALAY KAMPONG HOUSES

Kampong is a Malay word meaning "village". Traditionally, the Malays lived in separate dwellings grouped into kampongs which were separate social entities. The coastal and riverine Malay kampong house is very simply constructed with a rectangular pitched-roof shelter raised about two metres above the ground. The Malays place great importance on providing an elegant front reception area or *luar*, for entertaining guests during the Hari Raya festivities, at weddings, birthdays and other ceremonies, and where they may make their daily prayers.

*Above: The main living area of a Malay household. It is the social space where visitors sit down for conversation. At the back of the living area is the* tengah *which serves a variety of purposes. At night, if there are no partitioned bedrooms, it is the sleeping area. Mattresses and mats are rolled out, screens or curtains may be used to denote different family areas.*

*Left: Screens and mosquito nets provide privacy. Unmarried maidens of the house sleep in the attic, depending on the family organisation of the house. In the day, the mattresses are rolled up, mosquito nets dismantled and kept in a corner, often removed from sight by a folding screen.*

*Following pages: Different styles of Malay houses from the humble to the grand.*

# THE CHINESE VILLA

Wealthy Chinese merchants began to build their country villas about a hundred years ago, moving away from their shophouse to a healthier environment in their estates. Very much influenced by the Malay style house plan, these villas were double-storey, generally with a separate single-storey attached kitchen and servants' block at the rear.

Hiap Hin Villa built by Ong Kwan Hin, son of Kapitan China ("Chinese leader") Ong Tiang Swee, stands on a small hillock in his 12-acre estate. As a second generation Straits Chinese, born in Kuching, Ong Kwan Hin could very ably adapt the tropical Malay house for his large family of 10 sons and four daughters.

*Right: The airy room with coloured glass shutter windows is formally arranged with mother-of-pearl inlay blackwood Chinese furniture. An old English-made carpet covers the durian wooden floor.*

*Above: Ancestral portraits occupy a prominent central place in the hall. Ong Ewe Hai, the patriarch, made his fortunes in Singapore and extended his business to Sarawak in the 1860s.*

*Above top and right: In a quiet corner set apart as his study, Mr Ong Kwan Hin collects stamps and reads English books on poultry, pigeon-breeding and agriculture.*

*Above bottom: The front of the house, which resembles a Malay style house, is elevated on round plastered columns.*

*Below and right: The nyonya women of the house entertain their friends in a cosy nook. A marble octagonal tea-table is set with homemade rice-cakes using Straits Chinese porcelain. Imported Thonet chairs were fashionable as were the European carpets purchased from trips to Singapore.*

# CHINESE VILLA REINTERPRETED

The Chinese villas adapted from the Malay house quickly evolved into a hybrid architectural style merging with the colonial element of round lime-plastered columns that encased the original timber-stilts. A rather grand style emerged as the rich "towkay" merchants prospered and big parties were held on birthdays and festivals.

*This page: A goldminer's villa at Siniawan Bazaar has 10 bedrooms and a large family hall and courtyard. The shaded front open balcony on the first floor is a cool sitting space (top right). Wide shaded corridors link the bedrooms (right).*

## THE CHINESE FARMHOUSE

The Chinese who came to Sarawak to open up the land for agriculture built simple basic farmhouses. The floor is hard compact earth in all areas except for the bedroom which is slightly raised with timber boarded floor. The high thatch roof is steeply pitched to allow for heavy rainfall and to keep the interior space cool. The kitchen has space for a simple dining table, stools, an earthern hearth and mortar for rice-flour as shown in the picture on the left.

*Top and bottom: A family altar occupies central space in the main room while an old Raleigh bicycle and radio are exceptional luxuries in this farmhouse.*

# THE CHINESE SHOPHOUSE

The Sarawak Chinese merchants and traders were mainly Hokkien and Teochew from Southern China. The typical shophouse is a double-storey terrace house where business is conducted on the ground floor while the family resides on the first floor.

Early paintings and photographs of Kuching town showed shophouses on the Main Bazaar constructed of timber and *nipah* attap thatch roofing. Progressively brick and mortar and clay roof tiles were made and used as more Chinese settlers arrived.

Siniawan Bazaar, about 32 kilometres from Kuching, is still much the same as when it was built 70 years ago. All the buildings are of wood, and every trade that would service a rural community is found here – the grocer, butcher, barber, dentist, hairdresser and of course, the local coffee shop.

The area around Siniawan is also known for its caves with swiftlets that produce the famous bird's nest. Several shophouses are still involved in the business of processing the bird's nest, that is, removing the tiny feathers and cleaning up the gelatine-like emissions from the swiftlets' mouths before they become palatable.

*Left, top, centre and bottom: Timber shophouses were built in blocks of 10 to 12 shops in rows. Geomancy (feng shui) was an important aspect in considering the location of a building. Most shops therefore face the river as water is considered auspicious and, in real terms, very practical because rivers are the main means of transport in Sarawak.*

*Above: The front facade of this shop has louvred shutter windows and star-shaped accents.*

# TOWN AND TEMPLE

As the towns grew with the burgeoning Chinese population, specific trades began to be dominant along certain quarters and streets, which came to be named after them, e.g. Carpenter Street, Blacksmith's Lane, Pig Lane and Gambier Street.

Coming from their provincial towns in Southern China, the Chinese settlers brought with them their patron saints and gods, building temples of worship in their own architectural style.

*Left: The century-old Seng Ong Kong Temple faces a specially built wayang stage where classical Hokkien Chinese opera is performed on festival days. The Hokkien clan association, housed in a typical shophouse, is built just abutting the wayang stage.*

*Above: Rich Chinese merchants built large homes in the traditional Chinese style. The Chan Mansion is unique with its walled courtyards and a special three-storey tea pagoda.*

*Above: The old townscape of Kuching bustles with trading activity. Gunung (Mountain) Serapi forms a picturesque backdrop at sunset.*

*Right: The unique Seng Ong Kong Temple features an ornate roof with glazed ceramic tiles and handcrafted finials and ridge resplendent with dragons, phoenixes and mythical beasts.*

*Above: Kuching waterfront is always full of life with the traditional* tambang *or river taxis plying between the banks. These river boats have not changed since the time this lithograph (left) was made in the 1890s. Today, leisure boats moor at the banks as the river has become a popular venue for regattas and watersports.*

# THE ARCHITECTURAL DIMENSION — FOREIGN INFLUENCES

A hundred years under the rule of the Brooke "White Rajahs" has left a distinctive civic architectural heritage in Sarawak, particularly in Kuching, the seat of government. Buildings from the Brooke Era (1839-1941), which are now gazetted historic buildings, bear testimony to the British origin of the Rajahs.

After James Brooke had become Rajah of Sarawak in 1841, his energies were spent in establishing his rule. His nephew, Charles Brooke, who became the Second Rajah in 1868 was responsible for a number of important buildings, including the Astana, the Court House, Fort Margherita (named after his wife Ranee Margaret), the Sarawak Museum and the Pavilion. His son, Charles Vyner Brooke, succeeded him in 1917 and reigned till the Japanese forces occupied Sarawak in 1941.

The Brookes brought with them a style associated with rank, dignity and prestige which seemed inseparable from classical pillars and white stucco walls. In many ways this was adopted by the local Malay aristocracy and Chinese merchants who started to encase timber posts with brick and mortar. Whitewash was the common denominater of the "Datu's" kampong houses and the new villas of the Chinese "towkay".

Facades of the Chinese shophouses along the bazaars evolved from a traditional Chinese character to a hybrid architectural style combining Western neo-classical ornaments and arch windows with Chinese clay tile roofing and construction techniques.

What resulted is an eclectic style – a unique blend of East and West. The front facade of the Chinese shophouse is given a neo-classical Brooke style, but everything within remains totally ethnic Sarawakian Chinese.

In residential architecture, a peculiar breed of cross-cultural elements also evolved in what many scholars term "Sino-Malay-Palladian". This incorporates the Malay concept of an elevated dwelling with a Chinese tile roof over a Palladian elevation. Many wealthy Chinese businessmen built their grand country houses in this style as they move out of their residences above their shophouses.

Perhaps the biggest influence on the traditional architecture is the introduction of new building materials. The thatch and ironwood shingles are being replaced by metal-decking, and reinforced concrete will soon make timber structures obsolete.

The evolution of the Sarawakian architecture continues.

*Preceding pages: The majestic Astana home of the "White Rajahs" is still the official residence of the Yang Di-Pertua Negeri (Head of State). In the old days, the Astana was accessible from the town only by boat.*

*Left: Fort Margherita dominates the riverine landscape of Kuching. The grandest of a series of forts built by Rajah Charles Brooke along the lines of an English Renaissance castle, it is named after his wife, Ranee Margaret.*

# THE ASTANA

The original home of the "White Rajahs", the Astana is still the State Governor's residence. Built in 1870, it is reminiscent of an English country home with its brick pillars, whitewashed stucco walls and wooden framed glass windows. The high hip roof is of *belian* ironwood shingles. A ground timber staircase inside the original tower leads guests to a spacious lobby, before entering the grand Reception Hall.

*Above: Cosy sofas and wing chairs line the lobby. The original stucco friezes on the walls are oriental Chinese themes. Left: To add symmetry to the sole tower on the right, a new tower was recently added.*

*Opposite: The opulent decorative style of the Reception Hall reflects the current official taste.*

# BROOKE ERA BUILDINGS

The apparent Palladian influence of classical columns, pediments and white stucco walls was the predominant British colonial character throughout the region associated with rank, prestige and elegance. The Anglican and Roman Catholic missionaries brought their Renaissance style architecture which soon influenced other locals to build villas in the same manner depicting rhythm and order, proportion and scale based on European standards. The adaptation and improvisation using local materials and skills available were great architectural achievements.

*Above: Fort Sylvia in Kapit, built in 1880 of solid* belian *ironwood, has survived several floods.*

*Right: The Catholic Centre in Kuching has Renaissance style architecture.*

*The architectural elements of these buildings with their columns and colonnades testify to the Romantic Brooke Era.*

*Left and far left: An old mansion, now used as a school.*

*Below left: The General Post Office (1931), with its Corinthian columns, still bears the Rajah's crest and motto "Dum Spiro Spero" ("While I live, I hope").*

*Bottom left: The open space between the Court complex and the State Treasury is neatly paved and landscaped with trees, shrubs and park benches.*

*Below: The Pavilion (1909) was the first reinforced concrete structure built as a hospital.*

# THE COURT HOUSE

Wide verandahs and colonnades of Tuscan columns, evocative of Renaissance humanism, are the distinctive features of this complex of tropical buildings grouped around a central courtyard. Sir James Brooke, the first White Rajah, built this Centre for the administration of Justice in 1874. A Clock Tower at the front was completed in 1883 together with an addressing balcony made of iron grillework. The Charles Brooke (2nd Rajah) Memorial Obelisk, unveiled in 1924, is a granite structure with four bronze panels depicting a Malay, Dayak, Chinese and Kayan. The Rajah's marble relief sculpture is embedded below the coat of arms and crest of Sarawak.

The steep hip roof of *belian* ironwood shingles has lasted for over 30 years before needing replacement due to wear and tear. Honey-brown when new, they have now weathered to a warm grey-black.

*Left: Old and mature rain trees create a picturesque setting for the elegant Court houses.*

*Right and opposite bottom: The colonnaded complex of the Court House was raised about a metre above the ground to enclose a landscaped courtyard. The beautiful scale of the columns combines well with the lightness of the ironwood shingled roofs. Originally the corridors were also covered with solid* belian *planks, changed to tiles only 10 years ago.*

*Above: The courtyard offers a quiet retreat over lunchtime when the Courts are closed. The formal landscape reflects the civic nature of the building.*

## LANDSCAPE GARDEN SETTING

In a country of rolling hills, the early important buildings like the Sarawak Museum (1891), the Astana (1870), the Anglican Cathedral (1849) and Bishop's House (1850) were all built on top of hillocks. Well-trimmed grassy lawns and planned planting over the years have matured into green retreats and parks in the city today.

The character of the buildings are strongly European, particularly the Museum with its dormer windows and the quoined edges of the exterior walls.

Over the past century, bishops and curators have planted their choice of palm trees, frangipanis and hydrangeas, adding to the botanical garden character. The national flower of Malaysia is the red hibiscus. Kuching has adopted two official flowers: the yellow canna lily and the yellow allamanda.

*Above: At the Bishop's House, a pair of Honolulu creeper vines bearing pink and white flowers forms decorative archways to the spacious garden.*

*Left: Jacaranda trees shed their purple blossoms onto the well-trimmed lawns of the grand old Sarawak Museum.*

SO·ATI·ATA·PUAN·RINDU

# SPIRITUAL AMBIENCE

The early Anglican Churches were constructed in the simplest of tradition with available local hardwood. The Gothic arch and cross plan were elements that characterise the architecture. English bishops influenced the taste and order of things in the church. A spiritual ambience still prevails in the well-conserved structures.

*Left: A display of ancient Anglican commissary letters lines the walls of the Bishop's House.*

*Top and centre: Gothic arches at the Bishop's House.*

*Centre right, bottom: A watercolour of the interior of the Bishop's House, painted in 1849 by Harriette MacDougall, the first Bishop's wife.*

*Centre right, top: The grand wooden St. Thomas Cathedral, demolished in the 1950s, is now replaced by a masonry structure.*

*Opposite: St. James Old Church in Kampong Quop during early morning mass. Built in 1865, the church was constructed entirely of ironwood.*

# ATELIER BUNGALOW

This 1928 colonial building, nestled among *nibong* palms, "flame-of-the-forest" trees and fragrant *tembusu*, is the appropriate haven and headquarters of the Society Atelier Sarawak.

Beautifully decorated with the arts and crafts that the Society promotes, the Atelier bungalow is the home for artists and art lovers.

*Above: A giant clump of* nibong *palm dominates the front lawn of the Tudor-style bungalow.*

*Opposite: The bungalow's dining hall also acts as the Society's meeting hall. Potted begonias on old Bidayuh carved pedestals complement the archway. Iban-designed drapes frame the windows while paintings by Magdalene Tai are mounted on sieve trays.*

*Left: Specie-orchids and pitcher plants decorate the dining table set together with two Waveney Jenkins bronzes.*

*Above top: The upstairs' living room settee has pua-printed covers.*

# THE ARCHITECTURAL DIMENSION — MODERN CONTEMPORARY STYLE

Amidst the humdrum of modernisation, and the "politics of development" where new-age technology and materials become increasingly available in Sarawak today, a plastic pail is often easier to find in a remote jungle village than an earthern jar.

Sarawak people have gotten into the bandwagon with the rest of Asia in absorbing and assimilating Western influence and taste. Many nouveau riche would much rather boast of an Italian rococo settee than be proud of sitting on their finely woven traditional rattan mat.

Surprisingly, there are not many foreign expatriates living in the country compared to neighbouring Bali or Singapore. The modern contemporary style represented here has very much evolved locally, influenced perhaps by the people's Western education and their travel exposure.

The use of local materials such as wood, bamboo, rattan and other fibres plays an integral part in giving character to a Sarawak style. These may be left in its natural state, enhanced by polish or varnish, embellished with moulding and carving, or painted with the most brilliant of primary colours. In rural areas, modern longhouses continue to be built, more often of brick and concrete rather than the traditional timber or thatch because it is durable and cheaper to maintain.

The most visible feature of urban houses that reflects a tropical or Sarawak style is the high-pitch roof. No longer are the *belian* ironwood shingles commonly used because of the cost; instead coated tiles are preferred. In style, Sarawakian houses have become very eclectic, no longer displaying a pure Iban, Bidayuh or Chinese tradition but a combination, particularly in the interior decoration.

"More than less" may be an appropriate description of the ethnic love for "pattern-upon-pattern", the excesses of decoration often so profusely put together. The Iban and Orang Ulu costumes exemplify this idiom best, where the entire family's heirloom silver or beadwork is adorned for the occasion.

There is something about the Sarawakian way of amassing things of beauty and prestige, be it ceramic jars, beads, brassware, cannons, parangs, or deer horn. Collections build up into what some designers call a "clutter" style or a "fusion of confusion". Whatever one names it, the culturally minded parents, out of a hoarding instinct, would plan to pass down an heirloom or two to their children, especially as wedding dowry.

Ethnic tradition runs deep and will continue to translate itself into what we can visually see and appreciate. The culture, needs and values as well as the desires, dreams and passions of the Sarawakian become tomorrow's reality.

*Preceding pages: Wood and fibre – woven, plaited, natural or lacquered – are put together to form various patterned surfaces in the Ridu Farmhouse.*

*Left: A collection of spears, parangs and tribal jackets is displayed on a plaited bamboo wall of the farmhouse living room.*

# MODERN FARMHOUSE

Ten years ago when Datuk Robert Jacob Ridu (the first Bidayuh Speaker of the State Assembly) decided to rebuild his family's house on their ancestral land in Kampong Taie, he chose to incorporate as much of the local Bidayuh traditional use of building materials as possible, to show how these can still be attractive in a contemporary house.

With his artistic flair and clever interpolation of spatial arrangement, the mansion took shape, commanding a panoramic view over the rolling Penrissen hills, the family fishponds and farmland.

The airy terraces both at ground level and on the first floor evoke the traditional *awak* or open covered verandahs of the Bidayuh longhouse. High ceilings in the two main living rooms have open latticework that provide excellent cross-ventilation.

When the entire family gathers together for celebrations, mats are thrown over the corridors and verandahs to accommodate 500 to 600 villagers and guests.

*Above: A timber open deck with thick bamboo railings overlooks the family rice barn. Simple rattan furniture is used in the outdoor space.*

*Right: Shadows cast on the slate terrace floor create an interesting pattern due to the unevenness of the wild vine used for the lattice screen and arch. Traditional harvesting and storage baskets are decorative accents. The pair of ironwood chairs is a replica of the 1865 St. James' Bishop chair.*

*Above: The dining area features a 20-foot tall drum and other heirloom brass gongs. A grand old ironwood table serves well for buffet meals, but can easily seat 24 persons.*

*Right: Antique Chinese jars filled with wild flowers and carved Orang Ulu wood panels decorate the living room, reflecting the heritage of Datin Garnette Ridu, the Kelabit lady of the house.*

*Far right: The specially carved entryway to the family room has decorative Orang Ulu motifs of masks and shields.*

*Opposite: The spacious family room is a maisonette with a guestroom loft. Swivel rattan armchairs form a cosy area beneath lights of bamboo fish traps.*

*Left and far left: The journey up the smaller tributaries from the main rivers is exciting but tedious during dry spells and shallow waters. Then the longboats have to be pushed along in several stretches.*

# RUSTIC RETREAT

Way up in the upper reaches of the Batang Ai (River Ai) is a lodge built on the river's edge by Borneo Adventure, a local eco-tourism agency. The lodge serves as a halfway house for guests who travel to visit the Iban longhouse of Rumah Along at Nanga Sumpa.

Providing basic adventure traveller's amenities, the simplicity of the lodge exudes a certain charm. Open timber lattice windows all around allow for cross-ventilation. There are no doors to the bedrooms where mattresses are laid out on raised platforms, and privacy is afforded only within the confines of mosquito nets.

*Opposite, bottom: The lodge is built around a central open court of existing large* engkabang *illepe-nut trees. Decorative bamboo poles for ceremonies lean against the tree.*

*Right, top: Mosquito nets keep off the insects at night in the spacious bedrooms while pandanus mats cover the platforms.*

*Right, bottom: Wooden tables and benches are used for dining. A simple kitchen can be seen in the background. Old harvesting baskets are used for decoration.*

RUMAH DATUK ALFRED JABU

# IBAN FESTIVE SPLENDOUR

The stately home of Sarawak's Deputy Chief Minister, Tan Sri Datuk Amar Alfred Jabu ak Numpang, showcases the best of the tradition of Iban carvings. Specially commissioned ironwood panels from well-known Iban artists decorate the beams and columns of the Jabu's urban home. Being patrons of the arts and culture, Tan Sri and his wife, Datin Paduka Empiang, have a huge collection of carved hornbills and *pua kumbu* weavings. The house plan follows the arrangement of the longhouse with its *ruai* (common living area), *bilik* (private rooms) and *dapur* (kitchen). When family and friends gather and the *engkaramong* gongs are beaten, this urban longhouse comes alive with festive splendour.

*Left: Colourful carved hornbill icons used in the Gawai Festival decorate the entrance to the house. Vibrant primary colours are much loved by Ibans.*

*Right: Foliate scrolls on the carved panels have specific names and meanings. The beautiful chairs and table were made by longhouse Ibans who are experts in woodwork.*

TINGKUANG AK. SANGKAN. ENGKUDU. SEBITAN SARA TOK.

*Left: The formal receiving room for official guests features a three-panel batik painting by master artist Michael Lim. The prevailing theme of the hornbill is prominent in Iban legends and holds much significance for the Jabu's. Heirloom jars, brass cannons and kettles are special accent pieces.*

*Right: A corner on the terrace where a collection of drums is kept. Playing the* betabor *or "duelling drums" is a favourite pastime among the Iban community.*

# PAVILION OF ART

When Datuk Effendi Norwawi, a Melanau politician and entrepreneur and his Malay wife, Datin Farida, conceived the idea for their entertainment pavilion, they had a seven-sided polygon in mind, seven being his special number. "Enida" was built in 60 days to house their large collection of paintings, antique jars and brassware. As the Effendis are keen musicians, the acoustics of the pavilion was carefully conceived for their special evenings of music and songs.

The natural wood and stone character of the house exterior betrays nothing of the excitement and vibrancy of colours in the interior.

*Right: Several interesting nooks are created in the Pavilion for seating purposes as well as for displaying the collections of crystal, paintings and heirloom antiques.*

*Above: A huge carved ironwood ceremonial pole marks the Pavilion, acting as a focal point for the adjoining swimming pool.*

*Far left: The dining room is a burst of colours. The sparkle of crystal, candelabra and polished traditional* talam *food trays is a bold statement of the marriage of old and new. A framed silk* pua kumbu *decorates the end wall.*

*Above: An inlay panel of Arabic script "God is Great", set into a coral stone lattice wall, marks the direction of Mecca. The Pavilion is also used for prayer.*

*Left: Datin Farida's collection of old textiles and jars.*

# FABRIKO

"The luxury of Sarawak Style" is the banner of this lifestyle shop located in an old three-storey Chinese shophouse facing the Sarawak River and Fort Margherita. The natural colour hand-woven *pua kumbu* Iban textiles from the Fabriko weavers at Rumah Atong are exhibited on all three storeys together with other Sarawak art and crafts.

*Far left: The attic floor boards were removed and ironwood joists were exposed to heighten the top storey gallery which features antique and nouveau-designed Sarawak furniture.*

*Top: Old ironwood windows recycled for use at the ground floor boutique look into the staircase courtyard.*

*Centre and bottom:* Pua kumbu *are hung on old blowpipes and spears.*

# LANE BUILDING

The reconstruction of this three-storey shophouse along the old Kai Joo Lane by lawyer Yap Han Boon to house his legal practice was unprecedented. The jade-green glazed roof tiles and old Chinese style shutter windows breathed new life to an old Chinese quarter of Kuching previously noted for its opium dens and coffin shops.

*Far left: Marble-top Straits Chinese Peranakan tables are used throughout the office. An old Dutch dresser, Chinese jars and antique lithographs fill Yap Han Boon's private office.*

*Left: Replica bentwood chairs and marble-top table occupy the waiting lounge and library.*

*Above, top: The view out to the adjacent buildings is interesting. An old clerk's chair is recycled for use.*

*Above, bottom: A rear window looks out into a 1950s building with a spiral fire-escape stairs.*

# TROPICAL OASIS

Snug right in the heart of Kuching are the homes of the descendants of Kapitan China Ong Tiang Swee.

Mr Ong Kee Bian, his grandson and father of the author, built his bungalow house in 1958 in the style of the colonial government double-storey bungalows popular then. Originally the ground floor was open like a Malay stilt-house but extending family needs have created a tropical house with shaded patios. Over the years the garden has become a natural tropical oasis where exotic bamboos, ferns, anthuriums, heliconias and orchids thrive. Wooden statues and carvings peer out from hidden corners creating points of interest.

*Left: A mother and child statue from the remote borders of Sarawak and Kalimantan Borneo strikes a regal pose amidst yellow bamboo clumps.*

*Above and bottom left: Bidayuh* tegundum *pathway guardian figures find a natural home, well camouflaged with mildew and algae growth over the years.*

*Bottom right: The darker figurine set amongst pink anthuriams is a newer reproduction from Kalimantan Borneo.*

*Following pages: An open* belian *ironwood deck is shaded by de-barked* kayu seromah *poles under a fibreglass roof. Here, one can enjoy a cold drink any time of the day amidst plants, jars and tropical birds in the garden.*

*Above: In the living room,* pua kumbu *Iban weavings are used extensively for cushions, throws and table runners.*

*Right: The blue-grey silk covers in the family room is a new range from Fabriko. The carved sword-like display on the walls are weaving beaters for the backstrap loom. Rattan floor mats are Kayan-made.*

*Above: The antique oval dining table which is of beautiful teak wood is set with heirloom Japanese porcelain. Placemats are handmade sier reed from the Bakelalan Christians. Two* tikar burit *seating mats are centrepieces. Orang Ulu brass eardrops serve as napkin-holders.*

*Left: The family collection of Ming blue and white is displayed on the ancestral sideboard beneath a 1989 Michael Lim batik painting. Cut flowers are specie-orchids grown in the garden.*

# OUTDOOR THEME

An avid gardener and collector of heliconia plants, Mr Yap Han Boon set his house amidst magnificent rolling grounds of scented *tembusu* trees and tree-ferns. A small rambling brook runs in front of the house and under the entrance bridge lined with tall yellow bamboos. The house is tropical colonial style with prominent whitewashed columns on the terraces.

*Above: Wicker furniture with Fabriko-printed cushions are ideal for afternoon tea on the lawn.*

*Below and right: The timber deck over the rambling brook is a nice spot to enjoy exotic and wild fruits like the brown scaly* buah asam paya, *the pink* belimbing, *or the thorny sugar apples.*

*Opposite: Old colonial furniture are used on the terrace with old Chinese jars serving as decorative pieces.*

# NATURE SPLENDOUR

Surrounded by a housing estate, the owners of this double-storey house have created their own Eden-like garden courtyard, blending Western artifacts with native arts and crafts.

Several living areas are created, ranging from formal interior to casual outdoor spaces, each with the cosy personal touch of the owners.

*Right: Lush green plants create a cool courtyard. The timber gangway overhead links out from the master bedroom on the first floor. Pots of orchids and ferns are hung to create a jungle ambience.*

*Opposite, top: The library has a cosy patio where a set of contemporary cane furniture is placed. Treasure heirloom jars are displayed throughout the house.*

*Opposite, bottom: An "orangery" effect is created in the terrace living room which has a skylight. The beautiful floor mats are Bidayuh bark and rattan* tikar gelasah.

# PELAGUS RAPIDS RESORT

The Rejang River is Sarawak's longest river and the most treacherous, especially at the Pelagus Rapids, an hour's journey above the town of Kapit. Historically, the rapids also mark the territorial boundary between the Iban and Kenyah as set by the "White Rajah" during the Peace-Keeping Treaty of 1898. On both banks, the rainforests are thick and lush. The Pelagus Rapids Resort, located below the rapids, serves as a base for visitors to explore the Nature Reserve, and to make excursions to visit the native longhouses further upriver.

*Built on the banks of the Pelagus Rapids, the modern longhouse concept affords panoramic views of the river and the rainforest.*

*Right: The dining area has rattan furniture where one can sit and watch the boats go by.*

*Above: The upper deck lounge of the Pelagus Rapids Resort is good for lazing around on throw cushions.*

*Left: Boulders and rock outcrops in mid-river add to the danger of the rapids.*

*Left and opposite: All rooms at the Pelagus Rapids Resort have their own balconies either facing the rapids or the forests. Constructed entirely of timber, the railings and latticework with decorative carvings play on the light of the sun, creating interesting shadowed lights.*

*Right: A swimming pool set near the forest is a refreshing amenity at the end of a day's trekking.*

*Below: The main entrance doors at the Reception Pavilion of the resort are carved by Kenyah artist Tusau Padan.*

*Above and right: The Pelagus Rapids Resort buildings are linked by covered corridors which emphasise the spaciousness of the place.*

*Opposite: A central skylight in the main building features a flight of carved wooden hornbills.*

# SARAWAK VILLAGE BY THE SEA

The Damai Beach Holiday Inn Hotel overlooks the South China Sea and enjoys a magnificent view of the Santubong Mountain. The new wing of the hotel, built on the slopes of the hills, resembles a village of three communities: the Iban, the Malay and the Bidayuh. At the nearby Sarawak Cultural Village one can see authentic traditonal architecture from which these hotel chalets were inspired. The unique roofs of the conical *baruk* and pyramidal *lima* form interesting sculptural clusters against the landscape.

The interiors of these exclusive ethnic rooms are designed to reflect the culture and art of Sarawak people with special furniture and upholstery made to incorporate ethnic motifs. Covered walkways and stairs link all the chalets and rooms. Breathtaking views are afforded at any angle on the compound.

*Left: The round Bidayuh* baruk *chalets of the Damai Beach Holiday Inn Hotel have* belian *ironwood shingle roofs that weather to a muted dark grey. Lush planting and landscaping around the houses integrate the buildings into the forest panorama of the mountain slopes.*

*Above: Perched on the lower hills of Gunong Santubong, the new wing of the hotel commands a majestic view of the sea and mountain.*

*Opposite page: Various views of the Damai Beach Holiday Inn Hotel complex showing the blend of the wooden building forms and the lush landscape.*

*Above: Spread out on the hillslope, this modern interpretation of the longhouse is built on concrete stilts.*

*Left: Looking out of the Malay Chalet to the round* baruk *Bidayuh Chalets.*

*Left: The balconies of the longhouse suites are sunny and open. Carving motifs on the furniture are derived from the tribal heritage of the Iban.*

*Opposite, top: The Malay Chalet has traditional bird cages converted to hanging lights. The woven textile* songket *is used as wall tapestries, cushions and table runners.*

*Opposite, bottom left and right: In the longhouse suites, all ceilings are covered with tongue-and-groove natural-hued* bindang *timber panels. Other joinery and cabinetry are* nyatoh, *a smooth-finished timber. Traditional Orang Ulu baby carriers are mounted as wall decorations.*

*Above: The round Bidayuh Chalet is a suite on two levels. The lower is an open deck with a kitchenette bar. Floor tiles are patterned after designs on baskets.*

*Right: The swimming pool with waterfall is the place to watch the sunset over the Turtle Islands.*

*Left: The stairs to the bedroom on the upper floor is in the centre behind the traditional fireplace where an old jar is displayed. Walls slope outwards following the curvature of the roof. The bedheads have specially carved panels derived from traditional basket buckles while the bedspreads are specially interwoven with leather strips.*

*Below: In the jacuzzi bathroom, glazed mosaic patterns repeat the tribal hat decoration of Bidayuh priestesses. The decorative naive animals are carved by tribal children.*

# TRANQUIL LONGHOUSE BY THE LAKE

When a dam was built over the Ai River for a hydroelectric project, a huge lake was created. The Batang Ai Hilton Hotel now occupies a tranquil spot overlooking the wide expanse of water. The lakeside resort is a gateway to explore Iban country where several traditional longhouses are found by the rivers that feed into the lake.

Wide *ruai* corridors in each longhouse-type block lead to the *bilik* rooms, adhering closely to the traditional plan. The lobby and other dining areas enjoy a cool breeze from across the lake.

*Right and above: The sprawling blocks of longhouse overlook a man-made lake which has stunning sunset views.*

*Opposite, top: The* tanju *effect of traditional longhouses is depicted in the open balconies.*

*Opposite, centre and bottom: The bar lounge and room are enhanced by the warm hues of local timbers.*

# SARAWAK

## PORTRAITS IN BLACK AND WHITE

*Above: A gathering of Orang Ulu at Belaga during a regatta in the 1950s.*

*Opposite: Iban chiefs in their ceremonial dress. Their headdress is capped with a silver crown and complete with hornbill feathers and goat's hair. Silver necklaces, belts and armlets also symbolise their wealth.*

*"Soon after daybreak the people began to assemble beneath the great roof of the palm leaves that had been built for a conference hall. The Baram chiefs sat on a low platform along one side of the hall, prominent among them Taman Bulan, the most famous of them all, a really great man who made his name and influence felt throughout a very large part of Borneo. As the Tinjar men entered, the sight of their old enemies, the chiefs of the Baram, all sitting quietly together, was too much for their self control; with one accord they made a mad rush at them and attempted to drag them from the platform. Fortunately the white men had placed themselves with a few of the more reliable fortmen between the two parties."*

"Some 5,000 of the Baram people and the Madangs were encamped very comfortably in leaf and mat shelters."

"There was also a large number of Ibans, who more than all the rest are always spoiling for a fight."

# THE PEACE-KEEPING CEREMONY

In 1898, a Peace Meeting was held at Marudi (Claudetown) in the Baram District and in the presence of tribes loyal to the Brooke Raj, those tribes whose allegiance was still doubtful, and those who were still at variance with each other. The objective was to abolish old blood feuds and to persuade the tribes to aid the government in keeping the peace.

"Tama Bulan Wang, a great Kenyah chief who showed his true greatness by haranguing his people."

*Left: Charles Hose, the photographer for the pictures on this spread, was the son of an English clergyman. He was recruited to the Sarawak Civil Service as a cadet officer in 1884. Serving 23 years as an administrator, Hose was a keen naturalist and anthropologist. Above all, his photographic record of Sarawak and its people in the last century is invaluable as are his two volume books,* Pagan Tribes of Borneo *and* Natural Man.

*Left: The traditional life of the Iban was largely regulated by omens, particularly the way certain birds called and crossed one's path. But perhaps the most important form of omen reading involved the examination of the liver of a newly slaughtered sacrificial pig.*

# SPIRITUAL OFFERINGS

A *miring* ceremony is a common form of peace offering to the spirits. Plates filled with puffed rice, glutinous rice cakes and other delicacies are laid out in rows of seven. A little *sirih* (areca nut), tobacco, salt and a small helping from each plate are piled into a large plate together with eggs and a small cup of *tuak* or rice wine. The plate is then taken away and hung up in the rafters of the longhouse for the spirits to partake.

*Top right and below: Iban women love to invest their wealth in silver. On ceremonial occasions they wear as much of the jewellery as they can possibly manage.*

*Above: As part of the miring ceremony, the head of the longhouse, the* Penghulu, *waves a protesting chicken over the guests, invokes the goodwill of the spirit world and makes a graceful speech of welcome.*

*Right: Junaidi Bolhassan worked as photographer for the Sarawak Museum for over 30 years. His works form a valuable archival record of the Sarawak people's heritage and culture. The pictures on this and the following two spreads were taken by him.*

*Opposite: A Gawai Kenyalang or Hornbill Festival is celebrated in honour of Sengalang Burong, God of War. At the climax of the celebration, an elaborate carved hornbill representation is erected on top of high poles.*

*Recruited when small these two young girls have been ordained to be priestesses, and are already wearing their ceremonial hats.*

Right: *Two elder Bidayuh priestesses conduct a ceremony in the padi-field by sacrificing a white cockerel.*

# BIDAYUH PRIESTESSES

The spiritual life of some Bidayuh communities are controlled by priestesses who are spirit mediums. They wear specially tall seed-bead hats of conical shape. Some scholars believe that the peculiarities of the Bidayuh customs are due to a long forgotten Hindu influence. Hindu remains have been found in the Bidayuh areas. Certain of their spirit beliefs are reminiscent of the Hindu pantheon, and some of the Bidayuh sub-groups like to cremate their dead, again a habit which is unknown among the other peoples of Sarawak. A hundred and fifty years ago the Bidayuh were in danger of extinction; bullied and enslaved, they had no option but to allow expeditions of Iban to attack their areas.

*Above, top: The chief* dukun *or medicine man of the village in his full regalia.*

*Above, bottom: Bidayuh men perform a jostling dance demonstrating their martial prowess.*

*Left: Participants at the healing ceremony, which is attended by relatives and friends.*

*Opposite: Festival masks can look pretty frightful and are used to advantage by the boys to tease the girls.*

*Left: Palm fronds designate the area of ritual ceremony as the village elders sit in rows to pray and share traditional cakes and drinks.*

*Below: This Melanau matriarch had her forehead flattened by wooden boards fastened to her head when young. A broad flat forehead was considered a major beauty attribute during her time.*

# KAUL FESTIVAL

Once a year, the Melanau fishing community at Belawai hold a big Kaul Festival on the beach. The Muslim religious elders would lead in thanksgiving prayers on mats laid out on the beach before a meal is shared by everyone. The young people enjoy the carnival atmosphere of traditional games like riding on the giant swing called *tibau* and dressing up in fancy dress and masks like in a masquerade. Communal dances are also performed to the accompaniment of gongs and drums till twilight when festivities end, and everyone hopes for a more bountiful harvest of fish the next year.

*Left: The Melanau village with houses fronted by trampling platforms, on which sago palm flour is worked.*

*Above: The tattoos of Kayan women, done mostly on the lower arms, hands and legs, have fine intricate patterns.*

*Right: Iban men's tattoos have bold designs, and cover the legs, arms and back. Sometimes tattoos are also done on the front of the throat.*

# ETHNIC PORTRAITS

A gentle and gracious people, the Orang Ulu are at first shy and restrained, and many would run away from visitors or strangers, especially if they are equipped with a camera. With friendship and familiarity, they are exceptionally good subjects for portraits and exude a natural charm altogether, well deserving the "Natural Man" and "Noble Savage" titles so often used to describe them.

*Above: Beadwork is a special art among Kayan/Kenyah women.*

*Below: In the 1950s, tattooing was still very much practised among Kayan women as seen in this nurse and her patient at Sibu.*

*Above: Lim Poh Chiang, a Sarawakian photographer captures the honesty and integrity of Sarawak people through his lens in the 1950s and 60s.*

– *"The major portion of my photo collection was taken between 1953 and 1964, when I made over 13 trips to the Katibas and Baleh, the Oya, the Baram and the Upper Rejang rivers."*

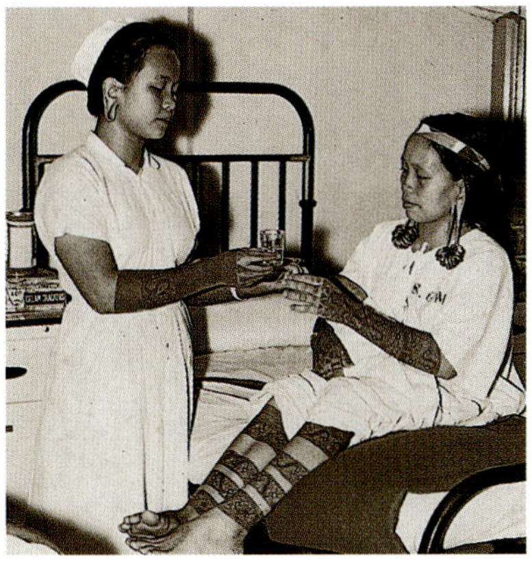

*Above: For women, child care and fieldwork are sometimes inseparable. This Kayan woman is going to the fields with a baby on her back. The delicate beadwork design of the baby carrier is believed to help ward off evil spirits.*

*Right: Kayan women stretch their earlobes with heavy brass rings as a sign of beauty.*

"Penan shelters are no place for the modern man. The raised flooring made of uneven tree branches is so uncomfortable, it would keep anyone from getting even forty winks. But to the Penans, like this family at Layun, it is the only comfort they know."

# THE NOMADIC PENAN

The Penan are among the last of the nomadic hunter-gatherers living in the remote forests of Sarawak. With their blowpipes and hunting dogs, they roam the forest in search of wild sago (their staple diet) while hunting animals, fishing and gathering wild fruits for their daily existence. Their skills in making blowpipes, mats and baskets are unsurpassed. Similarly, their knowledge of plant life, animal behaviour and jungle survival is unrivalled.

"It is arduous for the Penans to traverse the jungle. All belongings are carried on one's back. They continue eking out an existence in the only environment they are at peace with – the jungle."

"A young mother piggy-backs her sick child to the Long San Mission Clinic. Two years later, she herself died after succumbing to malaria. What has become of her little girl – I do not know."

*Above: Dennis Lau, a Sarawakian of Chinese-Melanau descent, captures shots that are revealing and unique to Sarawak. The photographs on this spread, taken over a period of 20 years from 1968 to 1987, portray a vivid impression of the Penan.*

"The Penans want development, but at the same time are not prepared to give up their nomadic way readily. To the Penans, the jungle across the river is always greener..."

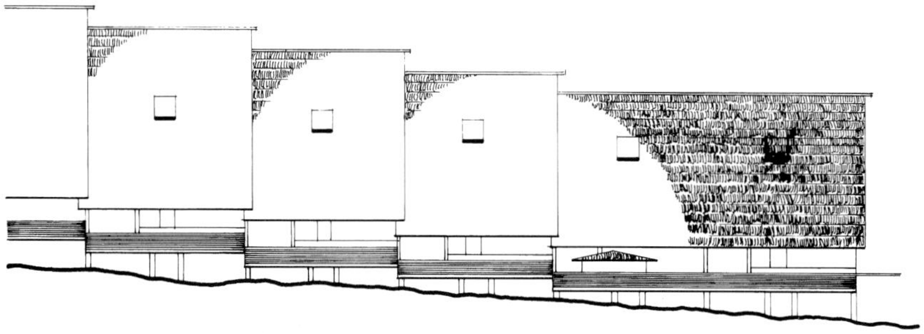

FRONT ELEVATION OF BIDAYUH LONGHOUSE

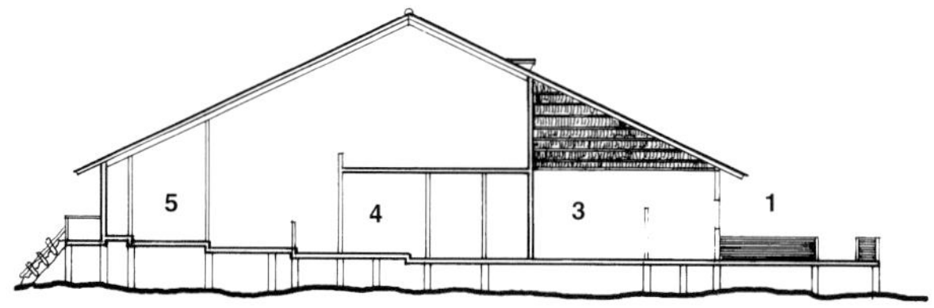


SECTION A-A

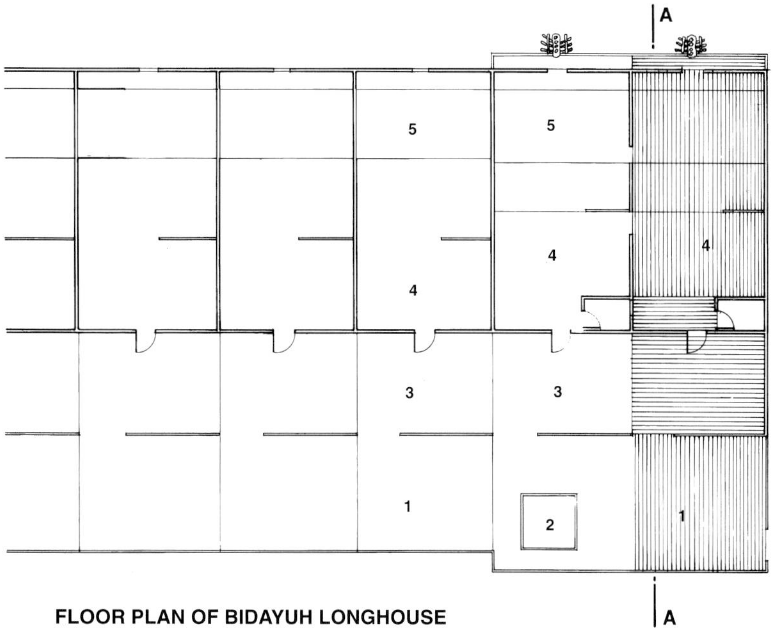


FLOOR PLAN OF BIDAYUH LONGHOUSE

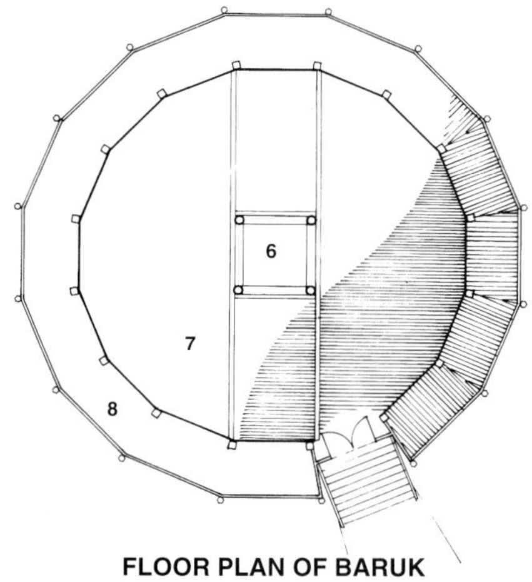


FLOOR PLAN OF BARUK

KEY
1. Gladak (Open Deck)
2. Padi Drying Shed
3. Awak (Communal Gallery)
4. Cooking & Dining
5. Padung (Resting Area)
6. Fireplace
7. Ceremonial Area
8. Raised Platform

## THE BIDAYUH LONGHOUSE AND HEADHOUSE

The Bidayuh longhouse is a series of family apartments all under one roof with a common communal gallery and a large open deck. Entry to the longhouse is by notched trunk stairs to the open deck and visitors would walk through this open deck to approach the individual apartment. The communal gallery is a semi-private space outside each *bilik* or apartment room. The Bidayuh example here is located at Kampong Gayu, Padawan area. The *baruk* or headhouse is based on the Kampong Opar at Bau District.

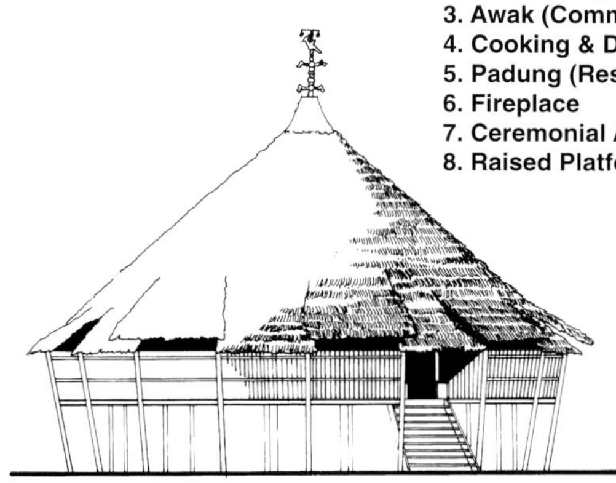

FRONT ELEVATION OF BARUK

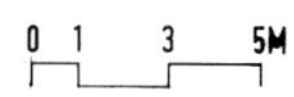

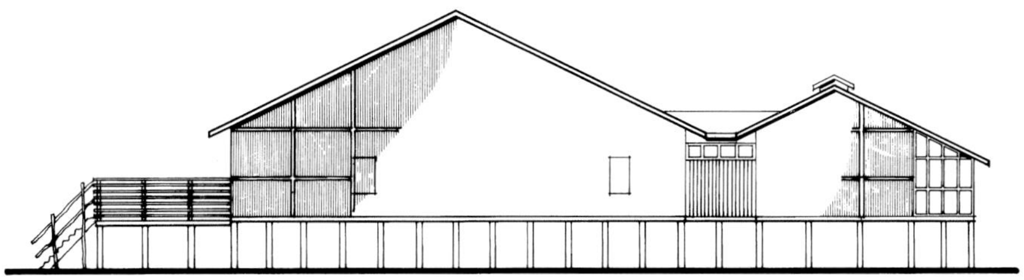

RIGHT ELEVATION

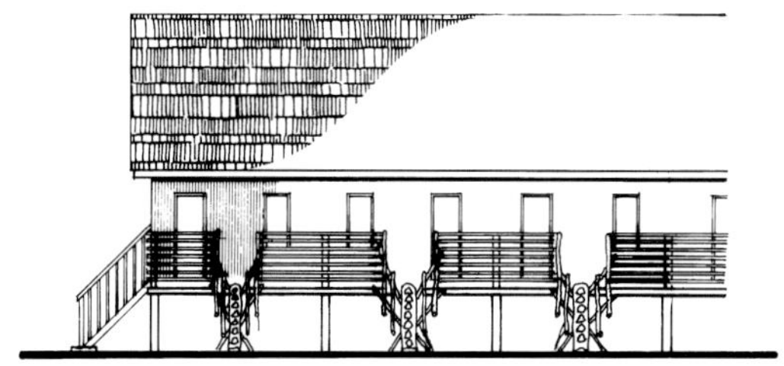

FRONT ELEVATION

## THE IBAN LONGHOUSE

The contemporary Iban longhouse is constructed with strong, sturdy timbers like *belian* ironwood or *selangan batu*. A secondary building at the rear houses the kitchen which is linked to the main house, forming an air well in between. The *bilik* or family apartments are all equal in size, and individuality is expressed on the front facade that faces the *ruai* or communal gallery. The example here is typical of the Betong-Saratok Iban areas. A variation of this plan can be found in the Rejang area where the building is raised a complete double-storey.

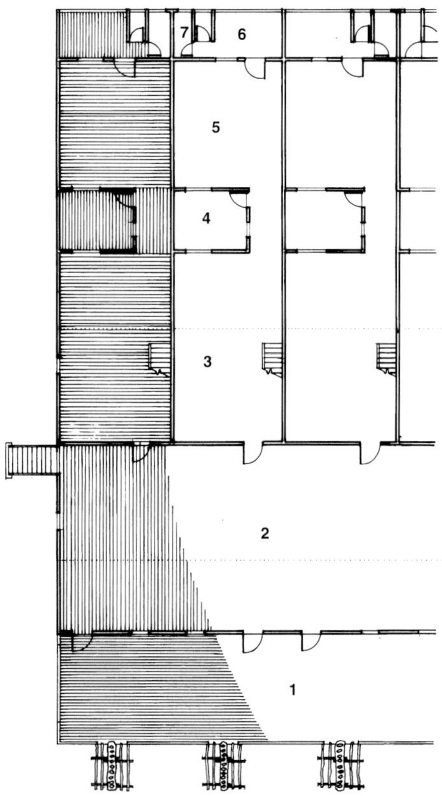


FLOOR PLAN

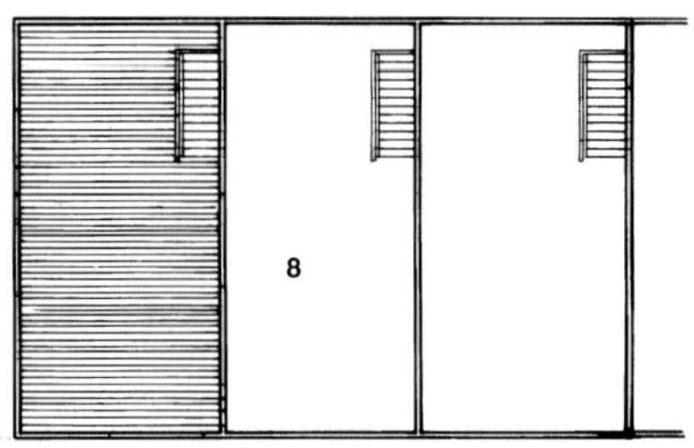


ATTIC FLOOR PLAN

**KEY**
**1. Tanju (Drying Platform)**
**2. Ruai (Communal Area)**
**3. Bilik (Apartment)**
**4. Air Well**
**5. Kitchen**
**6. Rear Verandah**
**7. Amenities**
**8. Sadau (refer to attic floor plan)**

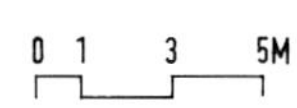

# THE ORANG ULU LONGHOUSE

The Kayan and Kenyah longhouses are similar in plan with the Chief's apartment, which is prominently located in the centre. It is larger than the ordinary family's unit and his superior status is often reflected in the raised roof over the rest of the longhouse and a larger verandah. Unlike the Iban, there is no open deck in front for drying padi and other crops. A small open deck is located at the rear beyond the kitchen. Rice barns are built by each family and sited away from the longhouse.

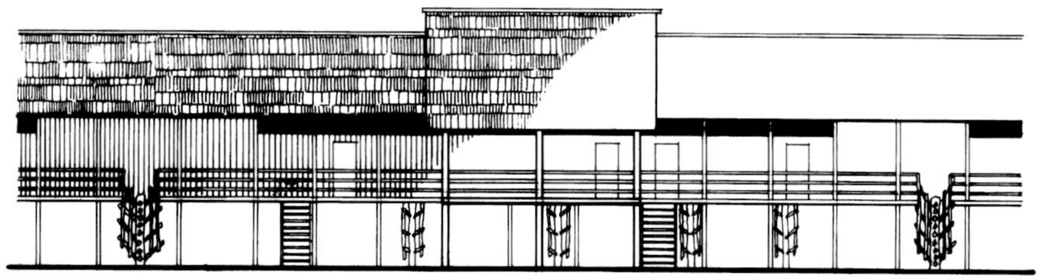

FRONT ELEVATION

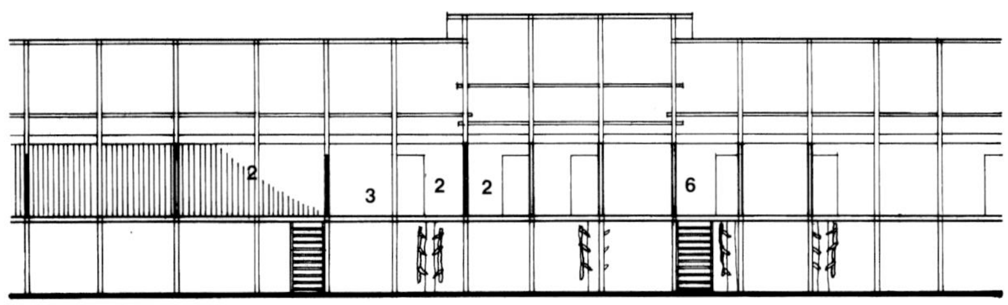


SECTION A-A

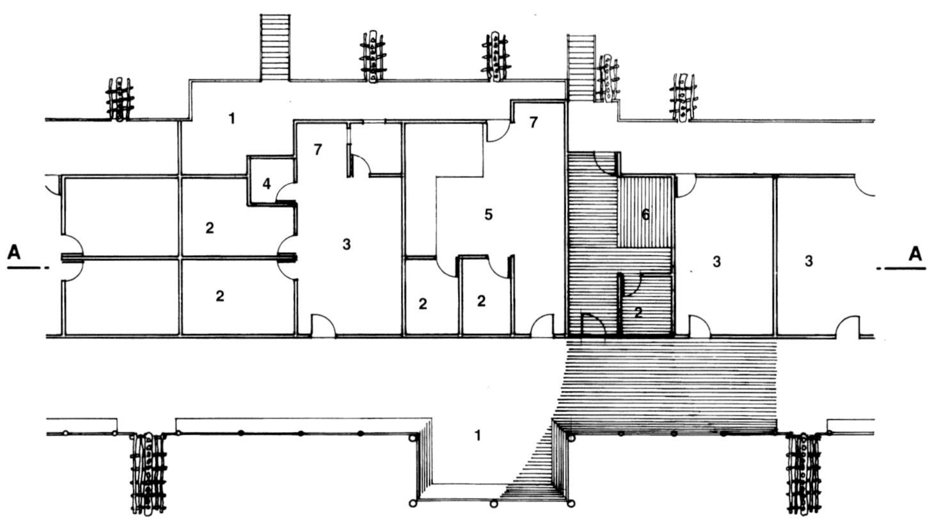


FLOOR PLAN

**KEY**
**1. Verandah**
**2. Bedroom**
**3. Standard Family Unit**
**4. Store**
**5. & 6. Chief's Unit**
**7. Kitchen**

0 1 3 5M

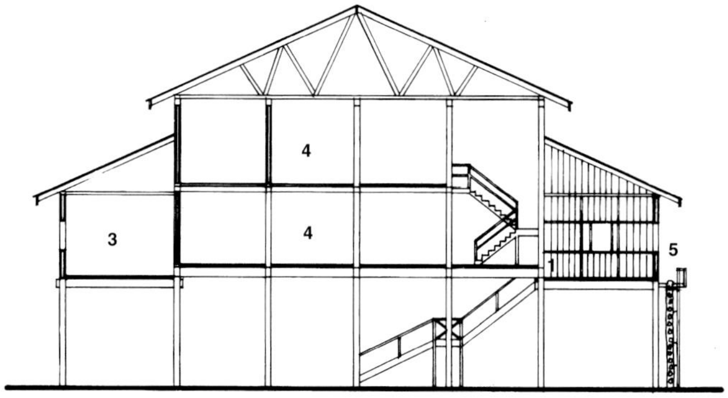

SECTION A-A

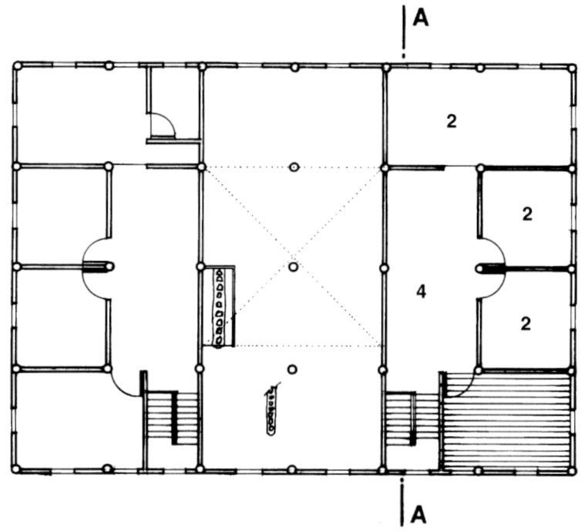

FIRST FLOOR PLAN

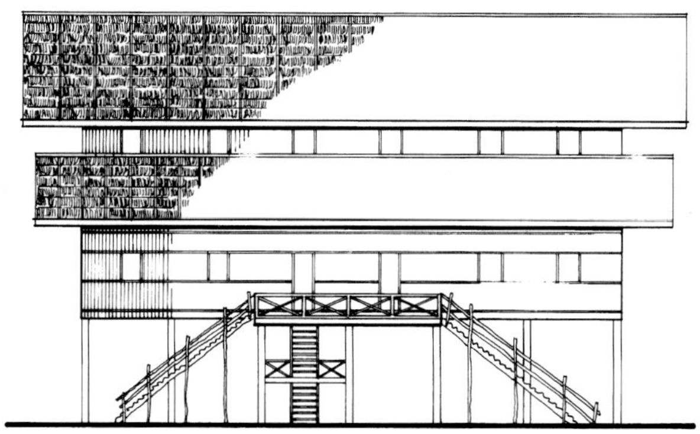

FRONT ELEVATION

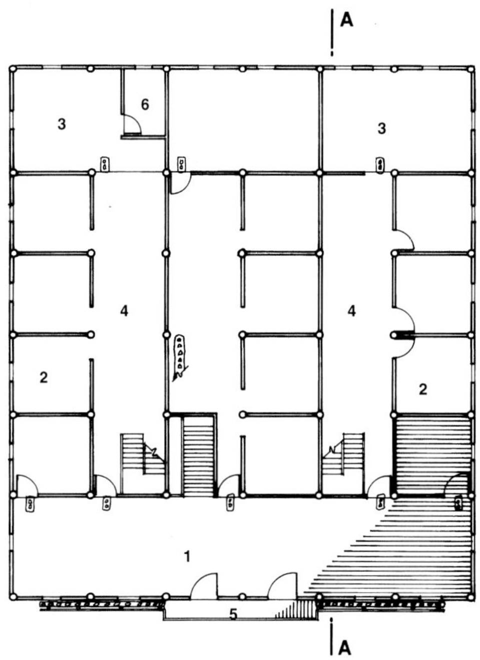

MAIN FLOOR LEVEL

**KEY**
1. Serambi (Communal Area)
2. Bedroom
3. Kitchen/Dining
4. Living
5. Balcony
6. Amenities

## THE MELANAU RUMAH TINGGI

Built on solid timber columns, the three-storey longhouse has walls of tree bark, flooring of double-layer palm trunks and *nipah* palm thatch roof. The front notched stairs can be drawn up for security against invading pirates and enemies. Three typical family apartments are shown in this plan, but usually there would be 20-30 apartments, each housing at least about thirty persons. Located along the coasts, this habitat is no longer built.

0 1 3 5M

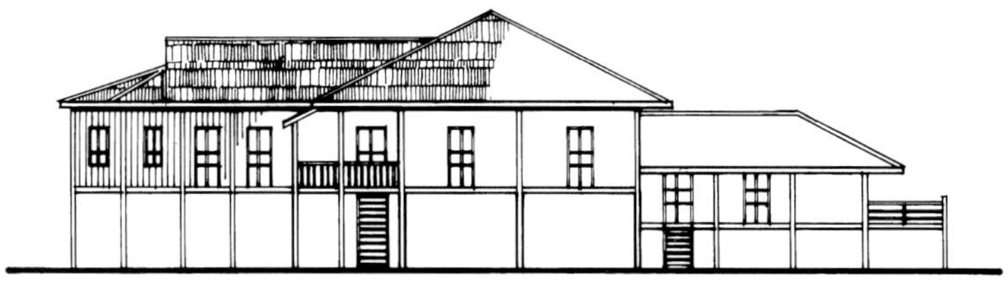

FRONT ELEVATION

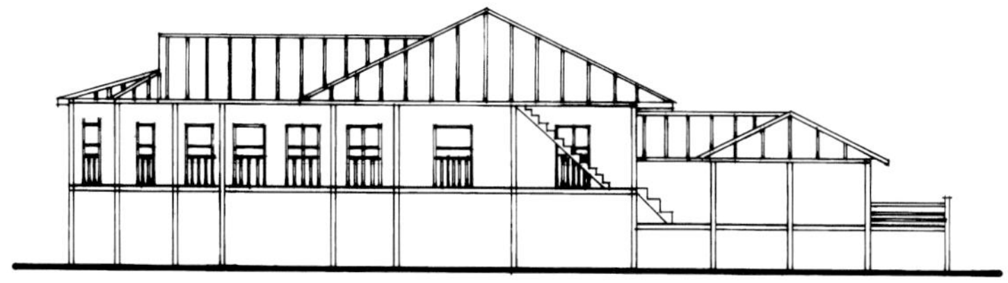

SECTION A-A

## THE MALAY HOUSE

The original Malay kampong house was a simple rectangular building with a kitchen annex at the rear. A later plan added a front living room or formal receiving room known as *luar*. The *tengah* (sleeping area) has no bedroom partitions but only screens and mosquito nets, making this an extended space for entertainment during weddings where the ceremonial dais is centrally located here. The *dapur* or kitchen annex is about two feet lower in level than the main building.

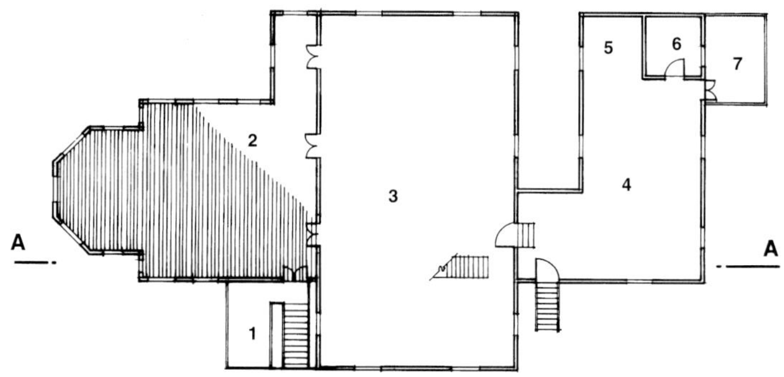


FLOOR PLAN

**KEY**
**1. Verandah**
**2. Luar (Living Area)**
**3. Tengah (Sleeping Area)**
**4. Dapur (Dining Area)**
**5. Kitchen**
**6. Amenities**
**7. Open Washing Area**

0 1 3 5M

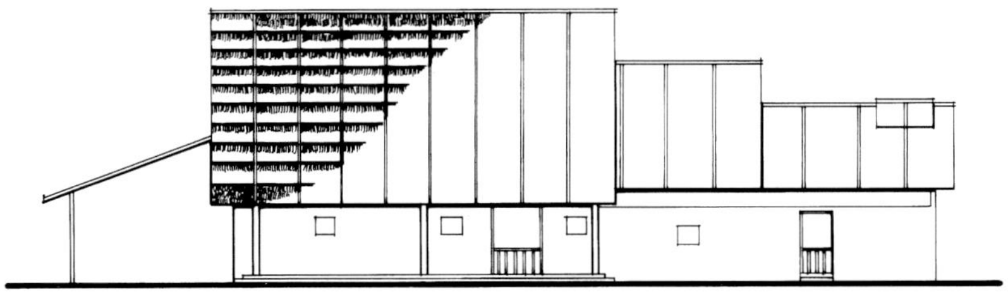

FRONT ELEVATION

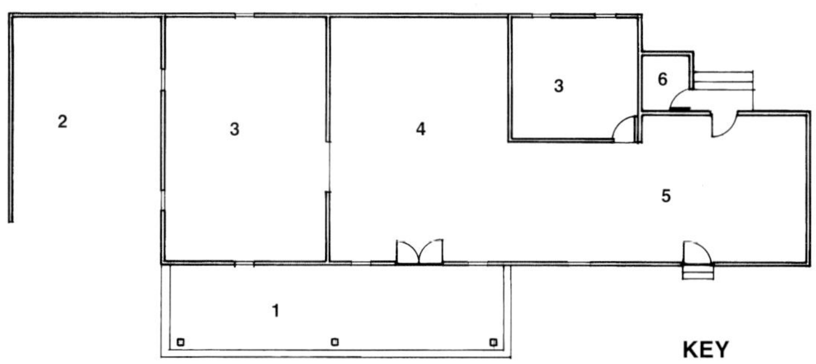


FLOOR PLAN

**KEY**
1. Verandah
2. Work Shed
3. Bedroom
4. Living
5. Kitchen & Dining
6. Amenities

## THE CHINESE FARMHOUSE

The simple palm-thatch pitched roofs broadly emulate the rural house in China. The important main house has a higher roof than the dining and kitchen. Built on hilly ground on the farmland, this Hakka house has an earthern floor, although the Foochow version is raised on stilts due to the land being swampy.

## THE PENAN SHEDS

Being temporary and erected quickly, these structures serve as shelters from the rain in the forests for a few weeks to a few months. Small tree trunks and branches are fastened together with rattan, a few mats are thrown over a raised platform which becomes the communal resting place.

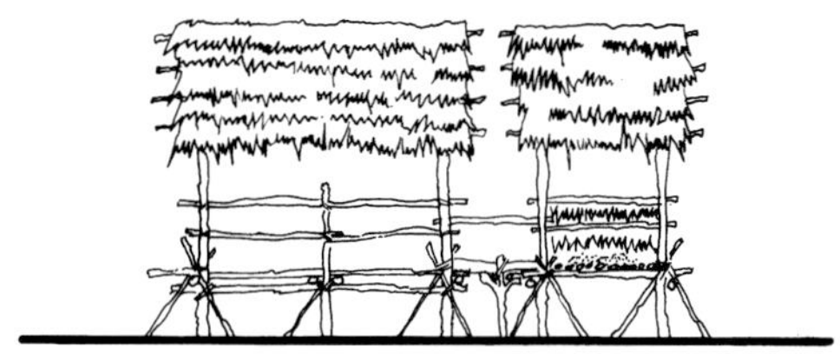

FRONT ELEVATION

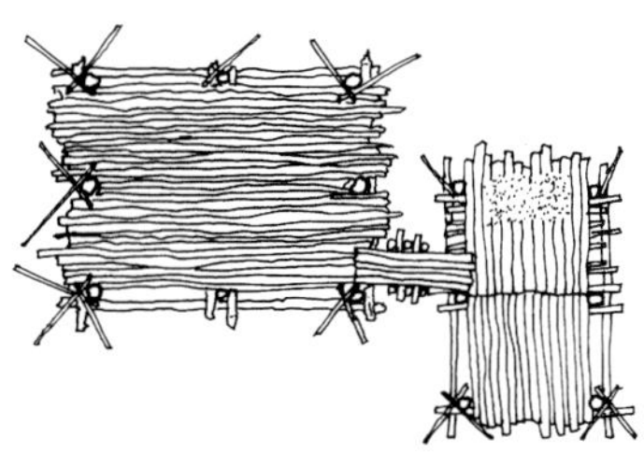

FLOOR PLAN

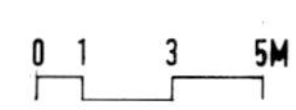

## IBAN MOTIFS (Recorded by Augustine Anggat)

**CARVED PANELS ON WOOD**
**a. Leaf scroll with flower bud**
**b. Leaf scroll with flowers**
**c. Leaf scroll with birds**

**SHIELDS**
**d. Pala Antu Gerasi (Giant's Head)**
**e. Chunggit (Sharp Tongues)**
**f. Kelindu (Fern Tendril)**

**PAINTED PANELLING**
**g, h, i. Variations of Ejabai Nguntai (Iban leaf design)**

a

b

c

## ORANG ULU MOTIFS (Designs by Kenyah artist Tusau Padan)

**a. "Tree of Life" wall painting with monkeys and leopards**
**b. Aso-dog door panels at Fabriko**
**c. Naga dragon door panels at Pelagus Rapids Resort**

a

b

c

d

# BIDAYUH MOTIFS ON BAMBOO

(From the author's collection)

**a & b. Incised paku fern scrolls on ceremonial sticks**
**c. Fern shoots design by Pa' Sijan for panelling**
**d. Ceremonial lime container design**
**e & f. Bamboo tubular containers with fern scrolls and zig-zag borders**

e

f